Pair-a-Dime Shift

A Special Educator's Forty-Five

Years of Reflection

Pair-a-Dime Shift
A Special Educator's Forty-Five Years of Reflection

DEBBIE WILKES

StoryTerrace

DEDICATION

After listening to the wisdom of an 8-year-old and the encouragement of his mother, Jamille I decided to embark on this venture.
This book is dedicated to my two daughters, Jamille and Beth, and my four amazing grandchildren, David, Mary, Harper, and Caroline.

Some names have been changed to protect the privacy of the individual.

PROLOGUE

"For it is in giving that we receive."

- St Francis of Assisi

I n 1970 I joined my fellow college classmates to visit Western State School and Hospital, an institution for the developmentally disabled in Canonsburg, Pennsylvania. We were all studying for our teaching degrees, but my passion was to someday help educate children with developmental disabilities.

As our bus trundled toward our destination, my mind went back in time to the day I met a young boy who had cerebral palsy. I was an eight-year-old Girl Scout looking to earn a service badge. At birth, the boy had suffered brain damage, resulting in a group of disorders that caused his muscles to weaken. He had difficulty with movement, and sometimes his muscles spasmed out of his control. He could not walk, so his parents carried him in their arms or he rode in a stroller.

When I met the boy, I knew right away that I wanted to do whatever I could to help make his life better. During our weekly visits, my job was to help him with "patterning therapy." In the 1950s the accepted theory of development for the "brain-injured child" was that stimulation was the key to unlocking a child's potential. A child could only progress if they met certain milestones in the proper sequence. Should a child with an impairment be unable to complete the "normal" stages of development, the belief was that the child would never graduate to the next level. An infant who cannot crawl will not evolve to their first steps, making it unlikely they will ever walk.

Today patterning therapy has been debunked by the American Academy of Pediatrics. In fact, many experts believe that the treatment was ineffective and perhaps harmful. Families were subjected to additional stress due to the high expectations for positive results. They were also spiraling financially trying to pay for the high costs of providing their children with this specialized treatment.

But back then, I was a young girl eager to help the boy strive towards a "typical" life. To steer him towards a day when he could walk across a room, I would gently grasp his legs, moving them in a walking motion. We would do this time and time again as the regimen was designed to cause muscle memory. I would slowly guide his arms upwards, making sure to avoid quick, jerky movements like the spasms the boy so often endured. Then I would help him to bend his elbows, holding his forearms and moving them as if he were crawling across the floor.

During those weeks that I met with the boy, I remember someone telling me that I was wasting my time. They declared that people like him were lost causes and should just be institutionalized. I had no idea what they were talking about. I had never heard of an "institution," not understanding that thousands of kids just like this boy were locked up inside these houses of horror.

Having seen with my own eyes how the boy was progressing, I ignored the naysayers, knowing in my heart that the time I spent with him was elevating his quality of life. In my mind, the patterning therapy would help him physically, and someday his world would become bigger—he would be able to leave his house, explore his neighborhood, and perhaps even go to his local public school.

The boy had a quick mind that was ripe for learning. He and I would sit for hours talking while I gently pushed his limbs to learn what they were meant to be doing. If only he could attend school with children his own age! I felt hope that maybe I could one day make a difference for kids who had limitations. Where could this lead, I wondered. Did I dare hope that someday all children, no matter their differences, could be accepted by their peers and just be friends?

On the day that I rode the college bus towards a building inhabited by hundreds of people labeled as handicapped, I was jolted back to those memories of the boy with cerebral palsy. I also flashed back to being told that people like him were useless to society and should be shut away. Within minutes I would learn first-hand the truth about these dismal places. The experience was profound and brought into focus how I would dedicate my life's work.

The bus pulled into the long driveway lined with thickly leafed trees shading a velvet green lawn that circled buildings resembling a college campus. I could never have imagined what was behind the sparkling windows. I stepped off the bus and followed my fellow classmates towards the impressive front doors. As we neared the building, I caught a whiff of stench that threw me off guard. My stomach dropped, and I felt like running back to the safety of the bus. But within moments we were ushered inside, and what I witnessed took my breath away.

Children and adults were scattered about the hallways, sitting against the walls, many of them wearing only diapers. Some moaned and yelled. Others looked catatonic, their eyes glassy, their mouths slack. The smell was overpowering, and my head began to swim. But even as the words screamed in my head that I couldn't do this, I knew I had to bear witness to this horror in order to change it. On that day, my determination to make a difference cemented itself into my soul.

Text Shelley Frost, on behalf of StoryTerrace

Design StoryTerrace

First Print March 2022

StoryTerrace

www.StoryTerrace.com

CONTENTS

1

CHILDHOOD 1950 - 1969

I was born in April 1952 in Milwaukee, Wisconsin, as the third of three girls. But when I was just a few months old, my family moved to Maryland, eventually settling in the town of Severna Park.

Janet, my oldest sister, was born in 1948, while my middle sister, Mary Jane, came along in 1950. Janet could not pronounce Mary Jane's name, so instead, she called the new baby Merdi (Murdi). To this day, my sister's closest family and friends call her Merdi as an endearment.

My older sisters remember my babyhood as a mixture of constant motion and exasperation. Merdi tells the story of a time when I was cooped up in my crib. I probably felt like I needed to burn some energy, but there I was stuck behind the metal bars inside a 2 x 4-foot prison. So, with all the power I could muster, I used the laws of physics and the rhythmic movement of my little body to make that crib roll on its wheels to the other side of the room.

Janet was four years older than me. Even though I

was the baby of the family, rather than ignoring me, Janet was my protector. Some of Merdi's friends liked to tease me, but Janet would always step in to save me from being picked on. Although she thought of herself as too old to play with Barbies, she would entertain me by playing with the dolls right beside me. She also had amazing sewing skills and she made beautiful clothes for my dolls. (Today, my grandchildren dress their own Barbies in those same clothes!) Because of Janet's kindness towards me and the natural way she understood my feelings, I idolized her. I also thought she was far prettier than the popular actress, Marlo Thomas!

When Merdi was born, the umbilical cord was wrapped tightly around her neck. The learning disabilities she dealt with as a child were probably a direct result of her difficult birth. A few years later, when I came along, my daddy saw me as the apple of his eye. I cherished being a daddy's girl, but this did not stop me from feeling jealous of Merdi. Our mother seemed to dote on her, whisking her away to mysterious appointments and leaving me behind at home. How could I understand that my mother had become a ferocious advocate for my sister? Her middle child was struggling with reading and writing. She also had delayed speech. In the early 1950s, the techniques used in speech therapy were relatively new and cutting edge. To give her daughter the best chances for a happy life, each week my mother drove Merdi to Annapolis, where she reaped the benefits of this new and effective speech therapy.

After moving three times before I was five years old, Cranford, New Jersey became my home all the way through high school. But early in my schooling, I began having trouble concentrating. It was not until 1968 that the American Psychiatric Association (APA) included in its *Diagnostic and Statistical Manual of Mental Disorders* (DSM) hyperkinetic reaction in children, which today is commonly known as attention deficit hyperactivity disorder (ADHD). From my memories and the way my family describes my childhood behavior, I very likely was a kid with ADHD.

Although my mother was strict with me, barely tolerating my whirlwinds of unfocused energy, when my teachers complained to her about my behavior, she became my biggest advocate too. One teacher pulled my mother aside and suggested that they put me on tranquilizers! My mother was outraged at the idea. She told her, "I've been able to help her for five years so you better figure out how to teach her. I am not putting her on medications!"

I do, however, remember one day when I managed to get on my mother's last nerve. Rarely would my mother pass me over to my father for punishment. But this time, she had had it, saying, "Your father needs to deal with you!"

My father took me by the hand and guided me upstairs into my bedroom. "My little baby," he said, using his pet name for me, "I'm going to hit the bed, and when I do, you start screaming." It worked like a charm, him swatting the mattress and me yelling my head off. I like to imagine that my mother knew full well what we were up to. She was a very loving parent, but my dad and I shared a special bond. He spoiled me something fierce, but his unwavering support of the person I was becoming gave me a kind of confidence and determination that carried me into my future years.

* * *

Our parents, Mary Jo and Jim Ray, raised us in the Catholic Church, but our religion was something we never discussed or evaluated. Just as the Catholic mass is filled with unquestioned rituals, our family went through the motions, never missing a holy day of obligation. Before each meal, someone at our table would say grace. And before bed each night, we said our prayers. If we were away from home on a Sunday morning, perhaps on vacation, my parents would manage to find a Catholic church so that we could attend mass. In those days, women and girls wore hats to mass. But if we were away from home and had forgotten our Sunday morning hats, my mother would place pieces of Kleenex on our heads.

Later, when I lived away from home for the first time as a college student studying to become a teacher, I would seek out the church. Dipping my fingers into the holy water at the church door entrance, genuflecting toward the tabernacle before sitting in a pew, and pulling down the kneeling bench and saying my prayers were like motor memory to my body. My conscience was unbothered by the infamous Catholic guilt people in my faith joked about. If I stayed out late on a Saturday night and missed mass the next morning, I would never feel bad about it. Faith for me at the time hovered on the back burner of my life, like an ancient redwood tree—solid, somber, beautiful, and timeless. But as I would discover in the years ahead, my faith in God and His guidance would set in focus my work to bring a higher quality of life to people with disabilities.

* * *

When I was eight years old, my mother's sister Louise gave birth to twin girls, Betsy and Barbara. From the moment I laid eyes on them, I knew they were mine. The adults allowed me to care for them, helping with feeding, bathing, and even diaper changing. Later, when they were in second grade, I even made their First Communion dresses. Every second I got to spend with the twins made me feel like I suddenly had a purpose in life. In fact, as they grew, my natural tendency to be an educator cascaded over the twins. Seeing them develop physically and watching their eyes alight after an accomplishment was so satisfying that I knew without a doubt my plan to become a teacher would come true.

But I was a poor student. My ability to focus and pay attention to my teachers was hampered by my ADHD. As much as I loved school, my mind would skitter off in a million directions, making it hard for me to digest lessons. Soon my grades went downhill. After a particularly bad report card, my mother sat me down. She said, "I know you want to be a teacher someday. But how will you get there if you can't do better in school?" She continued telling me that whatever choices I make now will put me on a trajectory to my future. The question was, did I want a positive life experience or something else?

I allowed her words to take hold of my brain. She was right. My dream of becoming an elementary school teacher would never come true if I could not figure out a way to absorb information. I gave myself a shake and made a promise to intentionally point my energy and focus on improving my grades. It worked. I taught myself how to ignore invading thoughts. I refused to give in to distractions. Instead, I consciously tuned in to the teacher's voice and the words she was saying. As my grades improved, my motivation increased. I graduated from grade to grade while self-managing my ADHD straight into honors classes.

Today I tell parents who have children diagnosed with ADHD that their child was born with a wonderful gift. ADHD gives a person a tremendous amount of energy. And should they find their passion in life, nothing will stop them from achieving their goals. Remembering how I corralled my own ADHD into a career that fulfilled my dreams allowed me to emphasize to parents the importance of self-advocacy.

While in school, something about my energetic personality drew in my peers. I was outgoing and talkative, and I loved being around people. I was friends with everyone in my class. The more people I met and learned about, the happier I was. But there was one girl, named Terri, with whom I shared a special bond. Terri was shy and reserved. When I met her, she really did not have any friends. I could see kindness in her, and I brought her into my group of friends. Terri gave me assurance. She could see that I had the drive to become a teacher one day. Even after we graduated from high school, going our separate ways to college, marriage, and families, Terri has been my very own Rock of Gibraltar – solid and enduring, helping me navigate the most difficult moments of my life.

One night in junior high when Terri was spending the night at my house as we were settling down in our beds, I pulled out one of my many books and began to read. Terri was not a big fan of reading, but I loved it. She would marvel that I would be reading more than one book at a time. Terri did not mind at all that I had my nose in the pages of a book while she was by my side. We could coexist in our shared space, respecting each other's strengths and weaknesses, knowing all the while that we were safe with each other. When I look back to those moments of childhood, I think that is how life should be for everyone. Where each of us has people who nurture our talents and act as a sounding board for us to figure out our dreams.

But my mind was becoming laser-focused. I had a fire in my heart to help anyone wanting an education. Those flames only burned brighter the day I met Dewy. I had joined my high school's Future Teachers of America Club (FTAC). My assignment as an FTAC member was to be a "peer helper" teaching Dewy how to read. Dewy was 20 years old. He was a big man with close-cropped hair and a magnetic smile. Despite his age, Dewy was still in high school. Kids were intimidated by Dewy. He was so large that when he walked into a classroom, everything seemed to shrink around him. To prove how tough they were, some kids teased Dewy. But his outlook was so sunny that even the worst bully could not ruin his day.

Looking back, Dewy probably had what was then known as "educable mental retardation." In the 1940s the terms "mentally retarded" and "mentally handicapped" were typical. People with these labels were further classified as educable, trainable, and custodial. A person who was deemed educable could be taught academic skills such as reading and writing. Trainable meant that a person could be taught basic life skills such as how to dress. Someone who was at the custodial level was presumed to be dependent on others and not given learning opportunities.

In the 1960s, while I was in high school, new terminology was beginning to replace these words. Although the label "mental retardation" was still used, the levels changed to *mild, moderate,* and *severe/profound.* Dewy most likely had a mild intellectual disability. Looking back, I am amazed that my high school provided Dewy with an education. He was mainstreamed before there were any laws requiring students with learning challenges to be given any consideration. The word "inclusion" had not even been invented yet, but there was Dewy in classrooms with his fellow students, making amazing progress.

I took my job seriously, regularly meeting with Dewy to go over his reading assignments. Soon he began having lunch with me, and he often joined me at other school activities including his prom. But it was in our tutoring sessions that I saw Dewy transform before my eyes. He would light up with joy each time he had a reading victory. I was excited watching him absorb my words, seeing him learning and gaining new abilities. I thought to myself that if Dewy had received specialized instruction when he was younger, the world of opportunities would have been open to him. I knew I was hooked! No longer did I want to be an elementary school teacher. I wanted to teach younger children. And I wanted to be a special education teacher.

2

COLLEGE 1970 - 1977

My grandfather, before he became a successful businessman, grew up on a farm in western Pennsylvania, where his family was poor and many of them uneducated. The country surrounding his home was all rolling fields and gentle valleys. The town he lived in was so small that any stranger who passed through was stopped and interrogated in the friendliest manner. When the construction of a railroad began nearby, my grandfather made it a point to befriend the surveyor. He was curious about the world beyond the peaks of the Appalachian Mountains rising in the south and the big cities to the east.

Very few of his friends and relatives completed high school, but my grandfather knew that education was the key to a happy, successful life. With ambitions to attend Ohio State University, he found a job teaching in a one-room schoolhouse. He saved every paycheck, planning to use the money for his college tuition. Later in his life, my grandfather described to my daughter Jamille, who had just gone through having chickenpox, a time when his little school had an outbreak of chickenpox. "I had already had Chicken Pox but I remember the students were feeling feverish and getting those blisters that turned into scabs. It was a miserable sickness. You want to know why we didn't close down the school?" he asked with a gleam in his eye. "Because everyone had it!"

Eventually, my grandfather graduated from Ohio State, and in later years, he held the prestigious job of vice president of the New York Central Railroad. When my grandfather was in his 80s, he moved to the city where I lived. We enjoyed a wonderful friendship and often had long conversations about life and our memories.

One day my grandfather wanted to talk about what I did for a living. I described to him the work that I was doing with my students—their array of diagnoses, personalities, and potentials. But my grandfather seemed to struggle with the idea that such a population of people even existed. He said, "People like that weren't there when I was a kid."

"Grandpa," I said, "People like that were there. They just got sent away."

My grandfather seemed to ponder that. Then he said, "I do remember children who were slow-witted. They staying on the farms to work."

At first, imagining any of my students being sent away to such a life made me feel sad. But after giving it a bit of thought, I said to my grandfather, "Perhaps that was an early sign of accepting and including children, but there were some who were still not included in all the other activities in the community."

* * *

In my family, it was no secret that I longed to be a teacher one day. But my mother had high aspirations for me. She was an early women's rights advocate and wanted her daughters to achieve great heights professionally. She herself had graduated from Cornell University and worked for IBM throughout World War II. But when the war ended, the men returned, and one of them took her job. For a time, she was a full-time homemaker raising her three girls, as was typical in the 1950s. But I believe that losing a job that had given her so much self-respect and identity in a man's world intensified her desire that her daughters should have high achieving careers. My choice to become a teacher was a bit too conventional in my mother's opinion.

I remember when, after I had narrowed my field to special education, my mother visited the school where I was teaching. There she saw with her own eyes my students in my classroom. She said to me with a note of frustration in her voice, "What's their problem?" Initially, I got mad at her for her thoughtless words. The students didn't have problems, they were created the way they were supposed to be. In an attempt to better understand, my mother would volunteer at my school, often acting as a chaperone when we took the kids on field trips.

In 1969, while a senior in high school, I searched for a university that offered a degree in special education. But there was little to choose from. The lack of higher education programs focusing on the needs of students with disabilities was telling. It was as if they were invisible to the educational system. It wasn't until 1975 that President Gerald Ford signed the Public Law 94-142, the Education for All Handicapped Children Act. This law was later reauthorized as the Individual with Disabilities Education Act (IDEA).

But I was aiming for a career that did not even yet exist. Finally, I learned that West Virginia University (WVU) in Morgantown offered a minor in special education. After I was accepted and declared my major in elementary education, I received a scholarship. During my years at WVU, I was fortunate to find a work-study job helping with research for one of my professors. But more than anything I was longing to get into a classroom filled with kids. But there I was in a very rural state where special education barely existed. As a student teacher, I was able to work as an "itinerant special education teacher." This meant that I would travel to provide education to students with disabilities. I remember walking over bridges and hiking through fields to reach the kids in my caseload. Most of these kids lived in abject poverty. Their homes were shanties, and their parents were unemployed. Although the hardship these families endured was heartbreaking, I will never forget what an amazing experience this was. My desire to make a difference for these forgotten children fed into my life's mission.

It was during my college years that I had the shocking experience of visiting the Western State School and Hospital in Canonsburg. Originally the building was a reform school for delinquent children, but by the time I stepped through its doors, it had evolved into a nightmarish reality for people with mental and cognitive disabilities. There were accounts of dehumanizing treatment of some residents and faculty over the years. What I saw firsthand, warehousing people with disabilities, shook me to the core and regretfully continues today. In that instant, instead of covering my eyes and running away, I wanted to be a part of the solution.

After graduating from WVU I received my Master of Education and my Supervision Certificate from Texas Woman's University. Years later in 2000, the Western State School and Hospital were permanently closed, and all the buildings were demolished. By then my work teaching and guiding students—who could once have been condemned within its walls—was making a difference.

* * *

During my undergrad years, I met Cecil, a sweet young man whom I began to date. It was my junior year, and our relationship began to blossom. After a few months, Cecil and I felt connected enough to become exclusive, only dating each other. I was flying high. My studies were fulfilling, my future was exciting, and I was with a wonderful boyfriend. But then in the summer before my senior year, everything changed.

Cecil was working a summer job as a flagman on the side of a highway near Wheeling, West Virginia. An out-of-control truck veered off the highway, hitting and killing Cecil. I was devastated. My senior year began, and it was all I could do to concentrate on my studies. Then I discovered a place on campus called the Newman Center. Specially designed for students of the Catholic faith, the Newman Center is a nonprofit organization that connects students to college ministries. In my case, although I did not seek counseling from the staff at the Newman Center, what I found was solace.

Years later, when I visited the campus with my second husband, David, I said, "Let's find the Newman Center." He had no idea what I was talking about since I had never mentioned to him the trauma I went through losing Cecil. But as we stood looking at the exterior of the Newman Center, I could remember how it helped my faith in God. My sense of prayer grew during that time, and it comforted me. The thought that kept recurring was, why? Why did Cecil have to die? That day I thought of my two beautiful girls and their children, my grandchildren. This was God's plan. For me, this was another turning point where I could see the immense value of my faith and the role the church has continued to play in my life.

3

EARLY WORK YEARS 1974 - 1979

I n 1974, as a freshly minted college graduate with a Bachelor of Science in elementary education, I was ready to hit the ground running. I had planned to work in the Washington DC area, but I did not have the money to start fresh. Back then, borrowing money for daily expenses was unheard of. I did not even have a credit card. My parents had moved to Dallas, Texas, so I decided to spend a year with them saving every penny I made.

One night I went on a blind date (I prefer the term 'visually impaired') with a man named Dave Wilkes. After our third date, I knew I was going to marry him. I soon came to realize that although Dave was a whiz at anything mathematical, he had dyslexia causing him to be functionally illiterate. But because of his wonderful, outgoing personality, people were drawn to him, perhaps explaining why Dave's teachers passed him from one grade level to the next.

Dave's ability to graduate high school without knowing how to read was another wake-up call on my road towards understanding the education system. I felt sure that if Dave had received intervention when he was a child, he could have grown to his potential. Without support from his parents or teachers, he was allowed to fall through the cracks. In later years, it was so clear how talented he was that I encouraged him to go to school to become a draftsman or an engineer. But he did not have the confidence. Despite this, as a father, Dave wanted nothing more than to spend precious time with his little girls. He taught himself how to read. Soon, each night while putting the girls to bed, Dave could read them a story.

While we were dating, I quickly saw that Dave had a heart of gold. Theresa was the teenage sister of a family member. She had recently broken up with her boyfriend. Her school prom was just around the corner, and she was devastated that she would be without a date. She called Dave and asked if he would take her to the prom. Without hesitation – or considering the cost of renting a tuxedo – Dave said yes. After the prom, Dave paid me a visit still wearing his fancy tuxedo. He described the evening including how he took Theresa to a pricy restaurant. Although I thought Dave's gesture of stepping in to help a friend in need spoke of his generous character that I had fallen in love with, the idea that they enjoyed a restaurant way out of our price range was a little irksome. But then Dave struck a pose like a model and said, "Don't you think I look good in this tuxedo?" There was a smile on my lips when I agreed that yes, he looked wonderful. "Well," he continued, "I think it looks so good on me that I need to wear it again. What about us getting married?" and then with a smile he said, "Oh by the way you do know that I love you and will love your forever?"

* * *

I was living with my parents and engaged to Dave when I began my difficult search for a special education position in the southern area of Dallas County. The Education of the Handicapped Act had just been amended to provide education assistance to all children considered handicapped. So, while searching for a job through school districts, I would see listings for openings such as 'Librarian,' 'Kindergarten,' and 'Music Teacher' but never 'Special Educator.' In fact, while applying for a job at one school district, I was advised that "those types of kids don't live here."

Finally, I was hired by the Duncanville Independent School District (ISD) to teach special education. The children in my classroom had never attended a public school. They had been relegated to a 'Children's Development Center' where they never interacted with "typical" children of the same age.

I felt excited yet confident as one of the first teachers to welcome these children to their first experience in a mainstream school. Before school even started, I felt inspired to write and design my teaching program. I had not yet even met my students, but I thought I knew everything. With all that I had learned in college fresh in my mind, I quickly put together a month's worth of lesson plans.

I will never forget my first day as a teacher. It did not go the way I had planned. By 10 a.m. I had gone through all my lesson plans. Later, two of my students went missing. When Mr. Crawford, the custodian, stepped into my classroom guiding two boys before him, he said to me, "These two must belong in your class." The day continued along that vein, and at 2:50 p.m., after I put my students on their bus, I returned to my classroom, dejected and teary-eyed.

Having been knocked off my pedestal, I knew I needed some advice. Two teachers, Claire Hurley and Gloria Key came to my rescue. Both women were diagnosticians and veteran teachers. Seeing how upset I was, they first affirmed me as a teacher, telling me that they believed in my ability and drive. We spoke at length about each of my nine students, none of whom had an Individualized Education Program (IEP).

But this was 1974, and assessments of students with disabilities were unheard of. It would not be until 1975 that the IEP program would be developed and used extensively in the public education system. Today IEPs are commonplace and have greatly enhanced educational opportunities and learning among students with both physical and learning disabilities. The beauty of an IEP is that a team consisting of school staff and the child's parents meets to review assessments of the child and to pinpoint specific areas of educational needs resulting from the child's disability. This

34

way, the child receives accommodations and modifications in the classroom designed specially to help them achieve learning goals.

Without the benefits of IEPs or any legal requirements fostering the education of my students, I was basically teaching in the dark ages of special education. But with Claire and Gloria counseling me, the three of us discussed their strengths and challenges and created specialized "IEPs" for each student. Throughout my two years at Duncanville, both women would become my comfort and my mentors. Twenty years later I reconnected with Gloria, who was an administrator at a regional training center for teachers. She recognized how her mentorship helped me to develop skills that led me to mentor others. The two of us came full circle that day when Gloria hired me to provide staff training at her facility.

Mr. Hardin was my boss and the principal at Duncanville. Regarding education, he had a progressive mind and was a true believer in inclusion. He understood that it was only common sense that "kiddos" with learning differences should be surrounded by "typical" children. He believed that integration would not decrease educational experiences for typical children but would in fact increase learning opportunities for children with disabilities.

Despite his forward-thinking leadership, many teachers at our school complained. They told me in no uncertain terms that they did not want my students on the playground while their students were outside. Just as my mother advocated for Merdi and me, I went to Mr. Hardin to speak on behalf of my students.

When he learned that some teachers were unhappy with my classroom's playground schedule, he said to his staff, "The kiddos in Ms. Ray's class must be outside with all the students. These students were brought here to be educated, and that includes playground time!" These teachers not only continued to object to my students being included at recess, but they also wanted them banned from art, music, and PE.

Those who complained about my students began to steer their animosity towards me. Somehow, they learned that I was originally from the north, so I was labeled a "damn Yankee." I did not help myself by using language that was misunderstood by native Texan fellow staff and parents.

One day Mr. Hardin called me into his office because he had received a nasty letter from a parent complaining about me. She claimed I had told my students they needed to spend money they didn't have to buy a bag for an upcoming field trip. Both Mr. Hardin and I were scratching our heads trying to understand what the parent meant. Then it registered. I had asked the children to bring a bag lunch, but what I didn't know was that the common term that I should have used was "sack lunch." Later my husband, Dave, bought me a dictionary of Texan slang words and phrases. It has served me well ever since. Years later, while providing a staff development in Duncanville I saw that the school where I began working, Central Elementary had its name changed to Hardin Elementary.

JASON

Jason was born with microcephaly, a condition where a baby's head is smaller when compared with babies of the same sex and age. For various reasons, a baby's brain may stop growing while in utero resulting in a smaller head size. Children with microcephaly often struggle with coordination, movement, and balance. But not Jason. He was the most coordinated, energetic, and athletic kid I knew.

Jason could throw and catch a ball perfectly. Whether it was a small tennis ball or a spiraling football, Jason had hands that could grab anything out of the air. If a jungle gym was in the vicinity, we would have to watch him like a hawk. He would tackle the bars, stairs, slides, and swings like a gymnast. And because he was so tiny, I could sweep him off his feet and swing him in the air.

While Jason was in my class, he made wonderful progress. When his mother hired me to tutor him over the summer so that he would not lose any of his new skills, she and I became very close. She confided in me that she and her husband were having problems. He was having difficulty accepting Jason, a child with a disability, as his son. Eventually, the father could no longer handle being in Jason's life, so the marriage ended in divorce. I remember feeling such anger at how selfish this man behaved. If I could have had words with him, I would have told him, "You were equally responsible for the birth of this child so get over it and act like a father!"

* * *

Although Mr. Hardin was a wonderful ally in fostering equality among our student population, he could not stop the unhappy mutterings of my fellow staff, who deeply disagreed with their boss. In my mind, the stance they were taking was dangerous to my students. A child who was subjected to this oppressive ideology would be robbed of their education. I was a new teacher in the mid-1970s tackling a job that had little foundational support in both a legal and a societal sense. I was pushing boulders up a hill. But my conviction that progress could be made in special education to benefit students who had been ignored was strengthened by my faith in God. He was nurturing my progressive beliefs, and I was not about to conform to the old ways of doing things. After two years of battling the attitudes of several teachers, I knew it was time for me to leave the school district.

I found a job at the Mesquite School District working at Angels Incorporated School that educated students with more significant needs from four surrounding districts. Although my building was separate from the general population of students, I loved it. Classroom management proved to be challenging, but through experience, I decided to focus on figuring out what the children were trying to communicate through their behavior rather than immediately resorting to discipline.

MIA

At this point, I was a newlywed, and my husband, Dave, was very supportive of my work. I was so fortunate that Dave understood the value of educating kids with special needs because I would often bring my work home with me. When I told Dave about a beautiful girl in my class named Mia with cerebral palsy, he stepped in to help solve a problem and improve her quality of life.

Mia was a delightful girl with a sparkle in her eye and a smile on her face that seemed to show her sense of humor. She was not toilet trained, but even though she could not verbalize, I knew she could learn this skill. Dave was a journeyman machinist, so after I described Mia and my belief in her abilities, Dave set his mind to finding a solution. He came up with a bell system that could be attached to the tray of her wheelchair. Once the bell was secured, I showed Mia how to hit the bell to let me know she needed to use the bathroom. Soon enough, she hit the bell and I took her to the restroom. After she urinated, I held for a while and said, "I am so proud of you! You are so smart!" Soon after, she hit the bell again, and I followed the same routine. On the second day of having the bell, she hit it 10 times! Clearly,

Mia had figured out that hitting the bell resulted in our cuddles and all my attention.

I soon learned that Mia was facing challenges at home and that she may need a foster home. Dave and I even discussed having Mia come live with us, but before we could finalize that decision, she was sent to a state school for children with cerebral palsy in Galveston. For years, I held her in my heart, wondering what had happened to her. Then one day that question was answered.

A few years ago, I was attending a transition conference. A speaker who had cerebral palsy was at the podium, and I remember being so impressed with her dynamic message and speaking skills. I turned to a friend of mine and said, "I would love to find out more about this woman." My friend helped to arrange a meeting. As we approached the woman to greet her, there before me was my precious Mia.

SAM

I was working in a career that I loved. There was never a different path for me. Teaching my students filled my spirit. But because so many of my students had compromised health issues, part of my job required me to follow doctor's orders. Sometimes these orders reduced the quality of life for a child. Whenever I found myself manipulating a child to fulfill medical requirements that caused a child to squirm and cry, well, to say I felt bad is putting it mildly.

While I was teaching for the Mesquite School District, I had a boy named Sam in my classroom who had continual seizures. To help control his seizures, Sam's doctor recommended that he follow the ketogenic diet (keto). The thought was that this protein-heavy and carb-free diet could be effective in reducing epileptic seizures in children.

Sam was a darling boy with a sweet nature. His easy-going personality made the task of feeding him the foods he was allowed only that much more difficult. Each day for lunch, I was required to open a can of Vienna sausages and offer them to Sam. He never took them willingly. At times I felt like I was force-feeding him those slimy, pale fingers of meat. I could only justify my actions by telling myself this food was important for his progress. But I knew these strong-arm tactics were taking away what was important to Sam – his dignity. The diet did not work, and his seizures continued.

* * *

When I chat with a grocery store clerk or consult with a salesperson in a dress shop, I think to myself, this is what I want for my students. I want them to experience everyday acceptance. My hope for them is that when they move through the world, people won't gawk at them or worse, ignore them. To just accept that we are all perfect at birth. We will share our similarities and compare our differences but how glorious would it be if people could simply accept that we are all just humans no matter our outward appearances,

41

our accomplishments, or struggles.

This idea that people are too ready to harshly judge based on first impressions became a problem in my personal life too. After Dave and I were married we bought a house. Having never lived together before our wedding day meant that we had a huge learning curve ahead of us. Our backgrounds and families were nothing alike. My parents were college-educated. His dad passed his General Educational Development Test (GED). Dave's mother referred to me and my family as "damn Yankees."

My parents had trouble accepting Dave. Dave was a machinist, not a college graduate. Although I wished my parents could have embraced Dave into our family, I could see that it would be up to me to show them what a kindhearted man he was. He made this easy. In those early years, whenever I needed a visual teaching tool, Dave would roll up his sleeves and using his artistic talents, would whip up colorful bulletin boards for my classroom. He also joined our field trips and later, became very involved in the Special Olympics.

Later, after we were married, I enrolled at the Texas Woman's University in Dallas to work on my Master of Education. I had earned scholarships to pay for my undergrad degree, so my parents generously stepped in to help cover the costs.

While working at Angels Incorporated, I became pregnant with my first daughter, Jamille. I always had a paraprofessional aid in my classroom to help me with lessons and activities. At that time, my paraprofessional was a woman named Gerry. Together Gerry and I would often do community-based instruction where we would take our students to learn skills such as ordering food in a restaurant.

One day as I was getting close to my due date, Gerry and I took our students to a Long John Silver's restaurant. While we were waiting in line, Gerry gave me a firm look and said, "What are we going to do if your water breaks?" I shrugged my shoulders having no clue what to expect. Then Gerry opened her purse and showed me a jar of pickles. I was long past those early days of having weird cravings so I could not guess why she thought I'd want a pickle now.

"Well," she said slyly, "If we are out and about and your water breaks, I'll just throw this jar of pickles on the floor!" It took a moment for me to register what she meant. To disguise a puddle of amniotic fluid, and to avoid my embarrassment, Gerry would save the day with her jar of pickles smashed to the floor. Then I said with a laugh, "Will people really think some jar of pickles dropped out of the sky?" But Gerry understood our classroom lessons – especially the one about protecting dignity.

4

HOME LIFE

I was pregnant with my first daughter, Jamille, and working at Angels Incorporated with students with severe and profound disabilities. I was over-worried about my pregnancy and was aware of each part of the gestation period knowing this is when disabilities may form. Time after time during visits with my obstetrician, I would query him about the development of my unborn child. Finally, in exasperation, he offered to perform a new test where some of my amniotic fluid could be taken to determine if my child had Down Syndrome. He then said, "What would you do with that information? Would you end the pregnancy?" I looked aghast and said nothing, I would never abort my child. She will be perfect because she is mine. With a smile, he said, "Debbie just relax and enjoy your pregnancy." And I did.

In the final years of the 1970s, I was a full-time stay-at-home mom. Dave was working hard as a machinist. Money was tight, and I longed to find a way to continue working with children with special needs. Some of the parents from Duncanville whose children were in my classroom had liked my approach to teaching. These parents advocated for me by contacting the Duncanville Parks and Recreation Department requesting that they create a summer camp program for kids with disabilities. The program was created, and I was hired to teach it. Although the camp was another wonderful opportunity to hone my skills teaching children who were my passion, it was not inclusive—in other words, "typical" children were not on my student rosters.

When my summer camp job ended another part-time opportunity became available. In 1980 the laws in Texas changed, ordering people who were living in institutions to be moved into group homes. Near my home, the Denton State Supported Living Center began to downsize its population of residents. This facility had been established in 1960, and by the end of that year, it was housing 1,700 adult residents. Along with 12 other state facilities, the Denton State School was established to provide full-time care for people who were medically fragile or who had developmental disabilities. The released residents were moved to community housing. To learn essential life skills, they attended classes at the Arc of Dallas, an organization that promotes, protects, and advocates for the human rights and self-determination of area residents with intellectual and developmental disabilities.

I was fully aware of the Denton State School and others

like it. These places are bleak institutions that are not fit for a prison. The standards are worse for these residents than what the prisoners had endured. It was at the Arc of Dallas where I found a job teaching night school classes for the ex-Denton residents. The students were adults, so the programs I taught were consumerism, shopping skills, cooking, and sex education.

My students who had come from Denton were wonderful, inquisitive people. They were so capable and willing to learn everything they could to help themselves become independent. As I watched them eagerly absorb the lessons, I thought to myself, "How in the world did they ever spend their time in that hellhole?"

My schedule at the Arc allowed me to care for my daughters during the day while earning money teaching at night. As my daughters grew from babies to preschoolers, I continued to relish being at home with them. I had no plans to go back to work full time until they were at least in kindergarten. But when the Arc changed the location of my night classes to a building in the Garland Independent School District, a new opportunity arose.

Each evening as I arrived at my classroom, I would take a few moments to chat with the daytime teaching staff. As we got to know each other, some of the teachers urged me to take a job as a regular staff teacher. But things had changed since I had left the profession to start our family. The state of Texas now required additional certification to be qualified to teach school. I felt the tug to get back into a classroom filled with the children I longed to teach. Even though my youngest daughter was still in preschool, I passed the test and found a job as a special education teacher at Garland Cooperative Training Center (CTC) teaching students with severe and profound disabilities.

But while my girls were still young, I wondered what we could do together as a family that would make a difference for kids with disabilities? I looked into volunteering with the Special Olympics, and before long, our entire family became deeply involved. My husband volunteered as a male chaperone, which was not an easy job. But it touched my heart that he took on this job and came to care about the kids he oversaw.

WILLIAM

During the Special Olympics, Dave and I managed the track and field events. One year, we had an athlete named William who I knew from my work at the Cooperative Training Center in Garland ISD. William loved to run and move, but he was unable to verbalize. One day, William had beaten us to the location of his next racing event. As the day wore on and William's event was delayed, I noticed that he got down on all fours next to me. Then he started to lick my leg.

Rather than jump away in surprise, I stood still, evaluating why William was doing this. In my work, I have often found that you need to be creative and accepting regarding the behaviors you encounter. I could remember my own hyperactivity as a child when my legs would sometimes shake uncontrollably while I was sitting in a church pew. My sister Janet assured me that the entire pew was shaking because of me! The lesson learned was that there is often a logical reason why someone behaves in a way that seems out of left field. In William's case, after a few moments of contemplating why he was licking my leg, I had my answer. It was a hot day and all of us had been sweating. William was licking the salt off my leg. He was harming no one, and I felt I understood exactly what was happening. Fortunately, I was able to find another way to satisfy his need for salt.

* * *

As much as the Catholic Church is a part of me, I sometimes found myself at odds with it. When my daughters were old enough to become altar servers, the church we had attended for many years was not allowing girls to have the honor of this duty. Knowing my family could not remain in an environment that was not progressive, we began attending St. Rita's, the Jesuit church where Dave and I were married. And that is where I met a man I would come to deeply admire—Father Schott.

I had been serving on the Parish Council at our previous church, so I thought it would be proper to introduce myself to our new priest, letting him know my family was now attending his church. Father Schott was so welcoming! He quickly set up a meeting with me during which he asked a startling question. He said, "Do you happen to know who Judith Snow, Marsha Forest, John Pierpoint, and John O'Brian are?" Of course, I knew those names. They were leaders in the movement for inclusion of students with disabilities.

I said to him, "Yes! I do know them, but more importantly, why are you asking me about them?" Father Schott must have known about my professional background, because he disclosed to me that he had a very good friend from the seminary whose grandson, named Luke, had Down Syndrome. And one month ago, Luke's parents had unsuccessfully applied for their son to enroll at St. Rita's elementary school.

Father Schott explained that St. Rita's school board was not amenable to allowing Luke to attend their school. Having heard about inclusion, Father Schott was interested in finding a way to convince the school board that they should admit Luke and that he should be included in regular classes. I could feel the swell of emotion in my chest, thinking of this little boy who was perceived as not good enough in the eyes of this school board. I knew I wanted to help Father Schott pull this board into the 20th century—with an argument that they could not deny.

I began by talking about abortion. "The Catholic Church opposes abortion," I said. "But what are we doing to support the children who were at risk of being aborted? Is it better to abort them from our lives before they are born or after they are born?"

"From womb to tomb," Father Schott agreed.

If his parents had learned that Luke had Down Syndrome in utero, they could have made the decision to end the pregnancy. But they brought their child into this world and into a church where the value of human life is of the utmost importance. Father Schott and I agreed that the church owed Luke an education.

At that moment I also felt something beautiful and strong embrace both me and Father Schott. I knew it was the Holy Spirit enshrouding us, as if telling us that yes, together we needed to advocate for this little boy. The next day Father Schott sent me a note saying how lovely it had been to meet me and that he could feel the Holy Spirit in the room with us. When I read his words and knew that he too had felt the Holy Spirit by our sides, my heart soared.

Within days I met with Luke and his parents. With Father Schott's support and my input, the St. Rita's school board reversed their decision and allowed Luke to enroll. He remained in the school through his eighth-grade year.

LUKE

Luke was a friendly, happy boy who grew into a responsible adult. He loved trying to help everyone and had a very engaging manner. This could make life difficult for him due to his language disability. Although he acted as if he understood what they were saying, he really did not.

He became a greeter at church, enjoying wearing his dress suit and tie. Later he got a job at Marshalls Department Store and attended a day program where I was on the board of directors.

Luke's parents are two people I deeply admire and respect. They provided a helping hand to their son without being overly protective. To help Luke become independent, they purchased a house that they wanted to turn into a group home for other young adults with disabilities. I was honored and thrilled when they asked me to help them facilitate the project. My role was communicating with parents of adult children who would possibly move into the home.

As the years passed, I continued to remain in Luke's life, helping to resolve behavior/communication issues and guiding him more as a friend than as a teacher. But what I will never forget is what Luke brought into my life—Father Schott and I encircled in the arms of the Holy Spirit.

* * *

My daughters had a close relationship with their grandparents. They called my dad, their grandfather, Papa Jas (pronounced 'jazz'). The name stuck because soon thereafter everyone in the family and close friends referred to my dad as Jas. Later, during the first decade of the 2000s, Alzheimer's began its cruel ravages on my father. I could see how this disease could strip the dignity of a person. This made me realize that, even if we do not have a loved one born with physical or mental challenges, we are all potentially affected by disabilities. In my heart I made a promise to everyone I served who lived with a debilitating condition—I will do whatever it takes to preserve your dignity.

Before he became sick, my father would spend a few hours each week volunteering at St. Paul's Hospital as well as answering the phone lines for the Alzheimers Association. When he learned of his own diagnosis with Alzheimer's my father's anguish was more about what we, his family would go through, rather than his own suffering ahead. We were forced to take away his driver's license, but he was able to commute to his volunteer jobs on public transportation. Even though we were nervous about him leaving the house alone, I felt it was more important that my father retain his dignity and continue volunteering. I dipped back into my educator's toolbox and came up with some ideas that would allow my father to fully live his life. We bought him a cell phone that was limited to calling just a few numbers. On the back of the phone, I placed a sticker on which I had written the steps to take to ask for help.

There were days when my father would be home alone for a few hours. He was not yet ready for a caregiver, but he did have difficulty communicating things that took place while my mother was out of the house. Should the telephone ring, my father would never let the answering machine kick in. He always picked up the call. My mother often went to church or bridge games but worried she might miss calls from myself, Dave, or my sisters. She would ask him if the phone rang while she was gone, but he was unable to describe who the caller was. I created a laminated poster with photos of each of us and our names written in bold letters. Each time my father took a call, he would just need to circle the name of the person on the other end of the line.

My husband Dave had a hobby of going online to research forgotten savings accounts, deposits, and other avenues of lost money. One day while he was investigating my father's financial past, he found some lost funds. Dave told my father the good news and assured him that he would track the money down. But my father became confused and convinced himself that Dave was trying to steal money from him! Using a visual strategy from my teacher's toolbox, I created a calendar. I told my father that the money should arrive in about six months. With the important day circled on the calendar, each time my father expressed frustration about the money, we would show him the calendar.

One day in a moment of clarity, after looking at his calendar and the laminated board my father said to me, "I don't know how you know how you come up with these ideas." I said to him, "Well Dad, the reason I know all this stuff is because you paid for my college education. You're the one who gave me this gift."

In his final year, my father was living in a facility for

people with Alzheimer's. One day a staff person called me to complain that my father was walking the halls without any pants on. No matter what they tried, nothing seemed to convince him that he needed to wear his pants outside of his room. I had an idea. While visiting my father, I helped him put on his pants and belt... backward. The staff asked me how I had figured that out. I thought to myself anyone could think of this solution. But then again, my professional life was dedicated to helping my students maintain their dignity using logic and compassion.

All my life, my father was the only person in the world who thought I was perfect. But it was I who stepped in to ensure his welfare as the disease wore him down. Often times my father became irritated with my mother, I was called in to play the role of the bad guy. Soon he began to call me "bossy" which I decided to accept as an endearment. But as the months rolled by, my father's lucidity and recognition of his loved ones lessened.

Then one night in October of 2009 while my oldest daughter Jamille was visiting, she asked to go visit Papa Jas. She understood when I told her he probably would not remember who she was. I had just been to see him a few days before and he had been so confused and angry having no idea that I was his daughter. As we stepped into his room, my father really looked at me. Then he said, "Debbie, where's your mother?" I caught my breath in surprise – he was lucid! Then Jamille said, "I'm going to get grandma."

Soon my mother, sisters, brother-in-laws, and grandchildren were all gathered around my father's bed. He knew everyone! We felt like a complete family again. We even brought in an entire meal that we shared together like old times. While we were all visiting, my father indicated that he wanted my mother to lay in bed next to him. After spending the entire day together and telling our father that we loved him we left. Later that night he died.

Looking back, I know those final hours when my father had come back to us, knowing all our names, reminiscing about the past – was a miracle given to us by God. To my father, I was flawless, a perfect daughter walking with God, changing the world one child at a time. When he passed away, the validation and unconditional love I received from him felt like it had dissolved into the night. But I feel deep gratitude to God for creating such a beautiful memory for my family.

* * *

I worry about the future and how people with disabilities will be included. I have faith that future generations can learn from the past. I have this faith because of my daughters. From the day they were born, my girls have always been around people with disabilities. While working at Garland Cooperative Training Center (CTC) I often brought my girls with me to dances and events held for my students. My daughters would see kids using wheelchairs, or nonverbal and drooling yet to them, the kids I taught were just kids.

As an adult, my daughter Jamille noted that the kids she met at my school were no different than all God's children. She never felt afraid or repelled by my students. She would watch me admonish them when they deserved it and hug them too. My students were held accountable because I had expectations for them. Jamille noticed that 'pity parties' were kept to a minimum.

My youngest daughter Beth has been a warrior since an early age when it came to correcting anyone who used improper language against my students such as 'retard.' Even when she was five years old Beth would admonish her cousins and other family members if she heard them using discriminative words about another person. She demanded that everyone use "person-centered language," meaning putting the person first and not the disability. She understood that a person with a disability is not a disabled person.

One day when Beth was in junior high school, she came home and told me a story that made me feel pride with a side of anxiety. There was a boy in her art class who had a behavioral disability. On that day their teacher singled out the boy and humiliated him in front of the class. To Beth, this was classic bullying behavior. Afterward, Beth approached her teacher and made a few suggestions. She told me, "I took my teacher aside and told her that her bullying behavior to the student wasn't acceptable. Then I told her if she needed strategies to help her be a better teacher in dealing with people with behavioral health challenges, that my mom was a specialist in the school district, and she'd be happy to help her."

After hearing this story and reaching down to the floor to pick up my dropped jaw, I felt hopefulness. My kids and their generation were already transforming the way people think and behave towards those with disabilities. The teacher did reach out to me, and for that, I give her enormous credit. Imagine being taken to task by a small girl, reflecting on her words then following through on her solution. It was remarkable.

When she was in high school Jamille volunteered as a 'Peer Helper' – students selected for their compassionate nature who kids could approach knowing they were in safe, non-judgmental hands. She became friends with a boy nicknamed Spider who was diagnosed with autism. He was so outgoing and friendly that everyone on campus responded to him. But Jamille became Spider's friend. They hung out together, having lunch or just talking like typical high schoolers. My daughter's empathetic nature encouraged me to believe that society was approaching a moment when people who are different would not be categorized or isolated any longer. Today, Jamille, along with being a wife and mother, works for nonprofits that provide services to those experiencing homelessness. She tells me that this is an often-misunderstood population. She learned while growing up that we need to serve and love people where they are. We may not have all the answers, but our efforts in their lives may help society take a second look at those who we often pretend are invisible.

One summer during her high school years, my daughter Beth was in a car accident. Thankfully she was fine, but her car was in bad shape. To pay for the repairs, she went out and got three jobs. One of those jobs was working for the school district as a 'job coach'. Beth would work with students during the summer helping them to become more independent in their jobs. She also developed friendships with them. Spider entered her sphere, and they became friends. Beth remembers being in a photography class with Spider and that he was very well-liked and popular with everyone. Besides coaching Spider in his job, Beth's duties were also to enable Spider in social situations including visiting our home. They would go to Chili's restaurant for lunch where Spider could practice conducting himself while ordering and paying for food. They practiced conversational skills which was a challenge for Spider, but he enjoyed the time together ordering his favorite plate lunch.

Later Beth worked at the same hospital where a student of mine named Matthew had found a job in the phlebotomy lab. Beth would tell me that Matthew was beloved by the staff and how reliable he was in his job. The staff had become very protective of Matthew, and they had proven their loyalty and respect for him. Today, Beth works in human resources. Recently she hired a young woman who she believes has autism. Her approach to working with all her staff including this new employee is to apply the same basic expectations - that they understand what their job is, and if they have questions, together they figure things out knowing mistakes will happen.

My girls have used words and actions to help people understand the giftedness of others

"No go, I will assist you in speaking and teach you what to say"

Exodus 4:12

5

THE STORY OF JIMMY COX

While chaperoning for the Special Olympics, my husband Dave became particularly close with a boy named Jimmy Cox who was a student of mine from Duncanville. Through the time we spent together at the Special Olympic games, Jimmy's family and ours developed a deep bond. I always thought that Jimmy's "light" helped both families show their love for each other and the lives of all the athletes.

Jimmy was born in 1962 to his mom Phyllis and his dad Jim. He was premature and a very tiny baby. His parents, still in their teens, suspected that something was going on with their newborn. He had fluid on his brain and at one month of age, Jimmy had a seizure. But it wasn't until he was nine months old that his parents were told he was born with Down Syndrome. Often a child with Down Syndrome will need heart surgery to improve oxygenation in their blood. Jimmy's pediatrician confirmed that he would require the surgery so that he could live past his first birthday.

One doctor who was in Jimmy's medical assessment group asked to speak to Phyllis and Jim as they were leaving a meeting. He painted a bleak picture of Jimmy's future. He said, "Your son may never be able to feed himself or dress himself. He probably will never have a job and he won't be able to speak." The doctor gave them a serious look and continued, "You should put his name on waiting lists of institutions for the mentally retarded."

Jim and Phyllis looked at each other stricken with the idea of sending their baby away for life. Jim said, "God gave him to us. We don't know how we're going to do this, but we are going to take care of him ourselves."

In the 1960s there were few offerings in the education system for children with special needs. Phyllis enrolled Jimmy in a preschool that was 30 minutes from their home. There she met a group of mothers whose children had a variety of disabilities. Together they formed a grassroots cause and lobbied the state of Texas to implement educational opportunities for their children. Phyllis felt a surge of hope when Jimmy was selected by a group of educators at the University of Texas at Austin who were developing one of the first curricula for special education. Jimmy and the other children in the group were pioneers! A film was even made to document this remarkable endeavor of creating educational opportunities for children who were often forgotten.

In 1974 when Jimmy was 10 years old, Phyllis and Jim

moved to Duncanville, Texas. On the day of his placement meeting with his new school administrators, Jimmy was in an irritable mood. He did not feel like answering questions and being under a microscope. The meeting did not go well. The administrator's decision of where to place Jimmy would be a turning point in his and his parents' lives. It turned out that I would be welcoming him into my classroom.

When she would visit her son's class to observe his progress, Phyllis and I began getting to know each other. She would remark to me how much joy I seemed to draw from my job. She also would observe my students responding to me and the way that I was teaching them. And my energy level! Phyllis told me that she had never seen anyone who worked with children have so much enthusiasm and passion that lasted throughout the day. I told Phyllis, "My kids teach me just as much as I teach them!"

Phyllis and my friendship blossomed. When I went into labor with my first daughter, Phyllis was by my side in the delivery room. As our families grew, our husbands and children became one big family. When Dave and I founded the local chapter of the Special Olympics, Phyllis and Jim joined as volunteers. Their son Jimmy was one of the athletes. His events were sprinting, shot put, discus, and his favorite – bowling. On the day the Texas State Special Olympics was held at the University of Texas in Austin, Jimmy's entire school attended the parade of athletes as they marched around the campus. Phyllis recalls that this was a 'red-letter day' for the athletes. For many of them, this was the first time in their lives they felt so important and valued.

During those years when the children were young, the Wilkes and Cox families often took vacations together. We would have beach days along the Texas coast, or we would go camping at lake communities where the kids could water ski. Dave and I would often have Jimmy stay overnight with us should Phyllis and Jim need a babysitter. Each time Jimmy saw me, he would joyfully throw himself into my arms.

Jimmy loved school and did well in his classes. He was very popular on campus. His younger sisters were known as 'Jimmy's sisters.' Jimmy attended both his Junior and Senior proms. On Senior Walk Day when each girl asks a boy to escort them as they walked in their formal dresses, Jimmy was asked by three girls to accompany them! As Jimmy got older, he gained confidence in how he spoke and expressed himself. For Jimmy, his school experience was wonderful. But out in the community, he was often reminded that he was somehow different.

Phyllis remembers a day when she and Jimmy were in a grocery store and Jimmy caught a mother and daughter staring at him. He said to his mom, "Why are they staring at me?" Phyllis said to him, "I don't know, why don't you go ask them?" Jimmy walked right up to the couple and said, "Why are you looking at me?" The woman and girl quickly turned on their heels and left the store. Jimmy watched them looking disheartened. He told his mother that he knew he was retarded. Phyllis said to him, "Honey, you were born that way. Just like I was born with freckles and blotchy skin. God made you and you're just fine." But being different meant that Jimmy had to work harder to be accepted. He was genuinely polite, holding doors for older women, saying 'please' and 'thank you' at the right moments.

When Jimmy was 16, it was time for him to undergo another serious heart surgery. After a round of tests, Jimmy and Phyllis sat in the doctor's office waiting to hear the results and the surgical plan. The head cardio surgeon sat behind his desk and took a hard look at Phyllis and her son. Then he said, "I can do this surgery for you, but do you really want Jimmy to outlive you?" Phyllis was stunned. Was he questioning the value of Jimmy's life? With fury in her heart, Phyllis took Jimmy's hand and told him it was time to leave. Jimmy was very intuitive, and he knew exactly what that doctor meant. Back in the car he wrapped his arms around his mother and said, "Mama, don't let that doctor operate on me." But Jimmy did have the operation – with huge success at the world-famous Mayo Clinic.

After Jimmy graduated from high school, he made the decision to move out on his own. He knew that he wanted to have a lifestyle that was just like everyone else's. And that meant he could not live with his parents. On the day Jimmy moved into a residence for adults with special needs, the sky was dark with clouds and rain pelted the car as they drove to his new home. Phyllis tried to hold back the tears that rolled down her cheeks. As she put her arms around her son to say goodbye, he stepped back and said, "Mom everything is going to be alright."

Jimmy found a job at the Southwestern University in Georgetown Texas working with an advocacy group. He told Phyllis, "Mom, I got a real job." Phyllis knew what he meant by that. This job was in the everyday workforce. He was side by side with 'normal' people rather than his previous jobs where his peers were his co-workers. Soon Jimmy figured out how to use the transportation services that took him to work and to the grocery store. He also found a personal trainer at a local gym that he joined. For many years, his life was the ordinary life of a young adult man. Then he began showing signs of Alzheimer's disease.

For reasons scientists don't yet fully understand, people with Down Syndrome are at a high risk of developing dementia similar to Alzheimer's. According to the National Down Syndrome Society, about 30% of people in their 50's with Down Syndrome develop the disease. People in their 60's have a 50% chance of having Alzheimer's.

Jimmy's decline into the disease was a very painful time for him and his family. Once a joyful, happy, easygoing young man, Jimmy now had irrational mood swings and often he would refuse to comply with his boss's instructions. Now in his early 50's Jimmy had been working at Southwestern for twenty-five years. He had even received special recognition for his many years of employment. Then one day while at work, Jimmy's reclusive sweet disposition returned, and ironically that was the day all was lost.

All his life Jimmy had had an affectionate nature. He was a liberal giver of smiles and hugs. That day at work, Jimmy was feeling good. His mood was sunny, and he was acting like his old self. While he was clearing dishes from a table, he noticed a girl standing nearby. He told her how pretty she was. Then he gave her a hug. She rebuffed him and reported his actions. Jimmy was fired.

The loss of his job had a profound and tragic effect on Jimmy. His confidence was shattered. He no longer had an identity. His job had made him feel accepted into the everyday world where his disability was in the background. Then, just shy of his 55th birthday Jimmy passed away.

Instead of a memorial service for Jimmy, his family held a birthday party. Family members one by one stood up to talk about the man who had been such a catalyst in their family. Unlike many families who crumble under the pressures of having a child with special needs, Jimmy was a magnetic force that tightened the bonds of his parents, sisters, and extended family.

On the day of Jimmy's 55th birthday party, there were tears mingled with laughter. People remembered him as a gentle soul who could not tolerate tension or arguments. Many stories were shared about 'Jimmy-isms' – funny sayings or words of wisdom Jimmy would impart to stifle conflict. Phyllis remembered a day when her husband Jim was at the wheel driving in heavy traffic. He was losing his cool and getting frustrated with the other drivers. Jimmy leaned over the seat and said, "Remember Dad, patience is a virgin."

As a nine-month-old baby, a doctor told his parents they should consider institutionalizing Jimmy. As a 16-year-old boy, a cardiac surgeon questioned the necessity of life-saving surgery for him. But Phyllis and Jim, now celebrating their 60th wedding anniversary, never let mainstream opinions get in the way of making sure their child reached his potential. Jimmy left behind a valuable legacy – having a disability does not diminish a human being. I think of Jimmy as a teacher whose lessons I use to this day.

With a family who believed in him, a teacher who educated and loved him, along with his own sheer will to live an ordinary life, Jimmy Cox was a man who broke the mold.

* * *

Because of Jimmy, the Wilkes and Cox families melded into one. When I gave birth to my daughter Jamille, Phyllis, along with my husband Dave, were my coaches in the delivery room. In loving tribute to the Cox family, we designed Jamille's name to honor my grandfather James and Phyllis and Jim's daughter Camille. "Camie" as we called her, had such a gentle soul and was a wonderful and devoted sister to her brother jimmy.

6

SPECIAL EDUCATOR 1985 - 1996

My grandfather was in his 90's and living nearby. My mother and I were his primary caregivers. Unlike my father, my grandfather did not have any age-related illnesses. I felt blessed to have him so intertwined in our lives - my girls called their grandpa, Gramps. He often came over for dinners and joined us on family outings.

During our dinners together my grandfather would listen to my classroom stories. Just as we cared for him, my grandfather did what he could to extend a helping hand to us. Dave's job as a tool and die maker was an endangered species. So much of his industry was being sent overseas often leaving Dave unemployed. When my high school reunion was planned in Cranford, New Jersey, we did not have the money for me to go. Without me even asking, my grandfather paid for my trip to go back east.

One night Dave and I went to visit my grandfather. While we were talking, my grandfather asked Dave if he was able to find a new job. Knowing how much my grandfather worried about us, Dave assured him that yes, he was working now. Later after we had left, I confronted Dave asking him why he lied to my grandfather. Dave was the salt of the earth, never had a lie crossed his lips. But he reassured me that this one time it was done out of love. He knew it would make my grandfather happy and at ease believing that our family was okay.

It was not too long after that my grandfather said to me, "Debbie, I've lived long enough." And just as he had been in charge of overseeing railroads and family finances, he was in full charge of his decision to leave this earth. He passed away at the age of 98.

* * *

During my time at Garland CTC, an incident happened with a boy student that rattled my confidence and made me question my abilities as a teacher. I wrestled with my conscience, asking if this was an innocent mistake or a complete failure of judgment. Even today when I reflect on what happened during that time, the sadness in my heart feels overwhelming. As the years passed, I found the silver lining—while coaching new teachers, I always told them the story of this boy so that they knew they too would make mistakes. Although I had the best intentions, the student at the center of my decision was traumatized.

He was a 16-year-old boy who exhibited a behavior that mystified the staff. Every day he would chew on tabletops. The tables were laminate, and he would bite them as if trying to eat them. The boy relished gnawing on the tabletops, seeming to find it very enjoyable. But the behavior was detrimental to his health—not to mention his teeth—so the licensed school psychologists came up with an idea to curb his behavior. Tabasco sauce would be poured along the edges of the tables. The theory was that he would place his mouth on the table and feel the burn on his tongue and lips, thereby convincing him to stop the behavior.

I followed through with the plan. The results were exactly what the administration had predicted. The boy's mouth felt the effects of the Tabasco sauce, and his reaction was heartbreaking. My reaction was dismay and shame. Looking back, I now understand that the boy had a great sensory need to grind his teeth on the table edges. What he was doing was not bad behavior. It provided him with the sensory feeling he craved. If only we had taken the time to evaluate the reasons why he demonstrated the behavior. We could have found a more acceptable way for him to feel the sensations he so desired and needed.

* * *

Although my fellow teachers such as Sharon Howard were wonderful to work with, CTC was a challenging place. I was disheartened at how segregated it was. Years ago, while working for Duncanville my students were better integrated because at least they were not sent to different schools. Instead, "retarded immersion" was practiced at

CTC. Sarcastically, I thought, "Just as learning a foreign language can be done by 'immersion' at this school, if you wish to learn how to be disabled or 'retarded,' just immerse yourself!"

In an effort to provide an opportunity for a more inclusive environment, my team teacher Sharon Howard and I took it upon ourselves to push wheelchairs and walk our students to a nearby high school where we had the Yearbook committee work with our students to put together the CTC Bulldog yearbook. This was a monumental achievement because we had to get permission from our principal and the principal of North Garland High School. The yearbook that our students created was impressive. Their work helped to change the way other high school students perceived their abilities. Regretfully, this practice ended after Sharon and I left CTC and took teaching posts at Lake Highlands High School in Richardson.

The prejudice against my students also existed in the community. I often organized my kids into a long line, making sure each had a partner. With Wanda, my para-educator (teacher's aide) at the rear of the line, I would take my students into town, where I would teach them about using money. One day we entered a restaurant to buy our lunch. Inside, lined up along the lunch counter, were several men wearing cowboy hats. As they stared at us, their faces were naked with distaste. Ignoring them, I assisted my students as each one decided what they wanted to order for lunch. Even though the rude stares continued, we sat at our tables enjoying our lunch and our accomplishments

JAMES

James was born with Lesch-Nyhan Syndrome, a genetic disorder that mostly affects male newborns. The effects of this syndrome can resemble cerebral palsy, but more specifically it can cause self-mutilating behaviors such as lip and finger biting or headbanging. James's lip and hand biting were so profound that most of his teeth had been pulled and his hands were always encased in oven mitts strapped down to the arms of his wheelchair. He was labeled as "profoundly retarded," but after getting to know James, I knew that was inaccurate. James's daily schedule included mornings in a "self-contained" classroom with special education students with profound disabilities and afternoons in my "semi-self-contained" classroom with students with less significant needs.

James's speech was labored and drawn out. His words were difficult to understand. This led some teaching staff to mistakenly assume that James could not comprehend their conversations. By the time James came to my classroom in the second part of his day, he often wanted to tell me what he had heard earlier from the gossiping teachers. I disapproved of gossip, but I valued James's dignity. I would take a chair next to him and listen to his stories. One day

James, having difficulty managing his tongue, said to me, "I lick you a lot." I gave him a huge smile understanding that he meant "like." The feeling was mutual. Later that day, when I told my family about James's statement, they were delighted, and in honor of James, from that day on we often used the phrase as an endearment to each other.

One of James's classmates was a tall, thin boy named Lucas. When Lucas walked into the classroom, he would swing his arms and legs as if needing all the space in the room. He too had a favorite funny phrase that my family co-opted. Whenever Lucas became excited or did not believe something he was being told, he would blurt, "Bull corn dog!" Ever since the day I told my family how Lucas used this expression, they too would say it when they heard something they did not believe.

When it came to my students, I often let the boundaries fall by the wayside. I knew that James was most relaxed when floating in a swimming pool. I would invite him and Sharon over to our house, where he could enjoy our pool. I would hold him in the water, and James would happily do his version of swimming. He and I would always have conversations, and I especially appreciated how creative James was in getting his point across.

One day James was telling me about his sister's boyfriend. But when he tried saying the boy's name, I could not understand his words. James got so frustrated that he blurted out, "Like an elevator!" A lightbulb went off in my head, and I said, "Is his name Otis?" James's face lit up, and I thought how clever he was to give me the perfect clue to make himself understood.

James and I had many conversations, but the one I treasure the most was when he told me how he envisioned going to heaven. Bluntly he told me that he would probably die before me. "Don't worry, though," he said, "I will be there waiting for you." I could feel my throat tighten as he described what heaven would be like for him. There, he would no longer be in a wheelchair. His hands would not be tied down, and he would be able to speak clearly. "The way you will find me," James said slowly, "you will see the love in my eyes."

* * *

The morale at CTC was disheartening. None of the teachers or administrative staff wanted to be there. When our principal, Dr. Price, got a promotion to work at another campus, we were saddled with a terrible replacement whose singular desire seemed to be to flunk everyone. My kiss of death was when Dr. Price advised his replacement that Mrs. Wilkes would "help with anything." At that time, I was a star teacher with an excellent evaluation. The new principal wanted nothing to do with the advice Dr. Price had left her with. Instead during teacher reviews, she singled me out, giving me a scathing evaluation. I could have been fired. I was not going to take this laying down, so I sent the evaluation to the Special Education Director. Everyone agreed that the evaluation was sorely inaccurate, which caused the new principal all sorts of trouble.

By then it hardly mattered, as I was approached by a woman whom I would later call "a profit in my life." Karen was a program specialist for the Richardson Independent School District (RISD). She recruited me to work for Richardson at the Lake Highland's High School. I brought with me, Sharon and Wanda. After I was hired, I worked in the district for the next 22 years.

7

PERSON CENTERED PLANNING

I t was 1988, and the work I would be doing at the RISD would become the foundation for the business I would start decades later. At RISD, once again I felt like a trailblazer and a destabilizer.

This was also the year that my friend Karen had a profound impact on my life and career. At first, we barely knew each other. In fact, I had interviewed with her in 1976 when I applied for a position at RISD. Today she and I laugh about those days because not only did I not get that job, but Karen did not even remember meeting me back then!

Karen had a daughter, Lauren with a disability, who received services through Special Education, yet she refused to have her labeled as "Mentally Retarded." Karen used to tell me, "Jars have labels, not people." Still, she was a tremendous advocate for special education and the children I was teaching. She recognized that I was a good teacher with new ideas and a heart filled with passion for helping to give these kids a productive future.

My first year at Richardson was also the first year in which people with intellectual disabilities were included in Lake Highlands High School where I was assigned. Not everyone was happy about this. I chalked it up to fear. The staff and students were unfamiliar with kids like my students, so their reaction was to balk and push back. Even our principal, Olen Pyles, was initially guarded when it came to accepting our program. But I learned that he himself had a nephew who was diagnosed with autism. Over time, he made the connection that our department and methods were of use to kids with disabilities, just like his nephew. For his Ph.D. dissertation, he chose to do an ethnography—the study of people and their cultures—he decided to focus on my class and our systems.

I was developing and teaching a program that emphasized work-based learning, teaching students to get ready for employment by actually doing real work at real work sites. Mr. Pyles was so engrossed in our ideas and how they would ultimately impact my students that he would often accompany them on the city buses as they rode to different businesses where they would practice their job skills.

It was critical that my students, now in their later teens, prepare themselves for the world that was just around the corner waiting for them. But as was often the case, some parents would get in the way of their child's future life by being overprotective. I could understand the angst parents of children with disabilities felt allowing their children to break free and experiencing the dignity of risk. From the day their baby is born throughout their entire lives, a parent is critical in the care and management of their child's health and welfare. But this sort of protective behavior can be damaging to a child with challenges. Studies show that children with disabilities whose parents dictate decisions and withhold opportunities can cause their child to lose their confidence. This can lead to the child becoming even more dependent and less likely to learn independence. They may feel isolated, lack a sense of belonging, and ultimately become angry and hostile towards their parents and others.

During this time, I had a student whose mother would pick and choose which part of the educational day she wanted her child to attend. Often, she would only allow her to attend the on-the-job training work sites, skipping the main school day altogether! I contacted her and told her that her daughter needed to attend all aspects of her schooling. The mother became very defensive and sought out the principal to complain about what I had said. She also took her complaint to the school board stating that I had threatened to shoot her daughter with a double gauged shotgun! After an investigation, instead of firing me, I was recognized for being an excellent educator.

It was after I survived that bout of parent unhappiness that the district selected me for the amazing opportunity at McGill University in Montreal. There, along with Bobbie, Karen, and other educators, I would be studying a growing concept in special education—inclusion. For two summers I lived in Montreal for two weeks, attending workshops and classes that emphasized the value of inclusion for students receiving special education. I was able to return to my school district with a new understanding of the many advantages of inclusion. Students receiving special education who are co-taught with their "typical" peers are absent on fewer days. Their math and reading skills become stronger. They are more likely to find jobs after graduation. Their classmates also experience the benefit of becoming more comfortable and accepting of people with disabilities. Friendships develop between classmates, bringing positive self-esteem for both typical and students receiving special education.

After what I had learned at McGill along with my own professional development and experiences, my approach to my job was becoming more progressive than some of the people I worked with. I was now a supervisor and Sharon, my teacher friend who came with me from CTC to Richardson, reported to me. Sharon and I were dear friends, and our families were close as well. Navigating a friendship that crossed from work to free time can be tricky especially when a philosophical disagreement bubbles up.

There was a time when Sharon and I did not see eye to eye regarding students in our program who were ready to graduate. Graduation for students with disabilities is based on outcomes that include full-time employment, attaining employment skills, or the ability to receive services that are not the responsibility of the school district. A final way to graduate is by aging out after their 21st birthday. In fact, this final method of graduation I used to call 'doing time.' The age of graduation for a typically developing student is eighteen. But students receiving Special Education services can remain in school through their 21st birthday so that they have the extra time to meet the graduation requirements.

But Sharon saw things differently. She argued that a student who continued in school for a few more years could develop and sustain friendships in a safe environment. I did not see the relevance of stunting a young adult's future. These were valuable years for them to build life skills that could support them and provide independence. The sooner their education was conducted into the real world with skills focusing on life after graduation, the better chances they had to transition into successful adulthood.

Then with the help of my colleagues Patty Fagan, Vicki Templeton, and Stacy Myers I was able to set up a transition program at a local community college. We were the only district in our state, providing person-centered planning as the foundation for the student's individual education plan. One of the first things we trained our young adults to do was how to understand and ride public transportation. Once they were proficient in that, they could enroll in college courses and be placed into jobs.

In 1990 the Americans with Disabilities Act (ADA) had been passed. No longer could businesses discriminate against a person based on a disability. The door to employment had been thrown open for our students. Now we just needed to find businesses with job openings. I began cold-calling big companies such as Target, Southwest Airlines, Presbyterian Hospital, and AMC Theaters. I also carefully evaluated the needs of my students to ensure that wherever they worked, the environment could benefit them as well.

While attending a program at McGill University in Montreal, Canada, I was exposed to a concept that laid the basis for the rest of my career—Person-Centered Planning. This is a creative way to empower a person to plan for their future focusing on and using support from family members and friends. The plan is built on individual strengths, gifts, and aspirations. It fosters meaningful and lasting relationships with family, friends, and community members and facilitates participation and inclusion in school, the workplace, and the community. Ultimately, the process is intended to provide an opening to their future and the world at large.

But one powerful point that I came away with from McGill was the need to drastically change the way we think about people with disabilities. I saw this as a huge paradigm shift and later when I provided training to parents and educators I made an impact by handing each participant 2 dimes when they entered the room. As an introduction to the session, I would ask them what I handed out. Some said "Twenty cents!" others said "Two dimes". I then put out

2 shoes and asked what they saw. Quickly someone would say "A pair of shoes". I then asked what each of them was holding in their hands and eventually I heard the response, "A pair of dimes! oh I know a paradigm." I tell them the paradigm shift is for them to not ask what is "wrong" with their child, but instead to look for their child's gifts and talents and not ask what the school district is going to do for them, but what they are going to do to make sure their child's needs are met.

* * *

Bobbie was an educator who was a wonderful influence in my life. She was an incredibly kind woman whose sense of calm could soothe a stormy sea, helping me to express my passion in a way that was acceptable to others. Bobbie had a memory bank that could recall important details to solve problems when I thought we were doomed. Bobbie was so wise in her approach to our mutual desire to raise the opportunities for children receiving special education that whenever I was in a quandary, I would ask myself, "What would Bobbie do?" It wouldn't take long until I had my answer.

One time Bobbie said to me, "Debbie, when I checked on your references, one of them said you were an agitator." Then with a twinkle in my eye, I retorted, "Only the agitator gets the laundry clean!"

For 10 years, she, Karen and several other educators and I created and ran the Southwest Institute for Inclusive Schools and communities modeled after the Institute in Montreal. During those years we brought together over 2000 people who spent one week every summer learning with experts including Judith Snow, Jack Peirpoint, Marsha Forest, Mary Falvey, Richard Rosenberg, Rich Villa, and many more. We were instrumental in helping people envision a world of inclusion and providing strategies to improve perceptions by people in schools, businesses, and out in the public.

At Richardson, Bobbie was my boss. Whenever I had a hair-brained idea, I would take it to Bobbie. Instead of putting up roadblocks, she would say, "Great! Now put a monetary value to it, and let's figure out the details."

Poor Bobbie – sometimes I really put that agitator to the test! On a regular basis, Texas Education Agency would review a school district's paperwork regarding compliance. In the late 1980s Transition became an area of scrutiny. I heard from coordinators in other districts who were changing their paperwork to make their district look like it was in compliance by holding brief IEP meetings to modify incorrect paperwork! Rather than worrying about being blamed for falling down on the job, I wanted principals and teachers to be held to a higher standard to meet the compliance standards.

A review was imminent, and Bobbie came to me asking that I check the paperwork to make sure all was okay. I flat out told her no, I won't do that. Bobbie asked me why I was refusing. I said, "If you force me to I will, but I want to show the agency that we are out of compliance because we are out of compliance!" Rather than worrying about being blamed for falling down on the job, I was more interested in having our district be given resources to correct our problems.

Sure enough, the agency reviewed our paperwork and deemed our district to be out of compliance. Suddenly, principals and other administrators began paying attention to the weak areas of our program. If we had handed in fudged paperwork, the substandard status quo would have continued. No one was fired. Instead, staff development became mandatory. This additional training we were receiving, in my mind, was all to the benefit of the kids we served.

Again, I put Bobbie to the test when I and another colleague, Vicki Templeton, approached her about creating a model of using person-centered planning with students in high school. Over the years I found that my students, while enrolled at school, could become employed, yet when they graduated their options and opportunities were minimal. Many parents shared my concerns. They were justified in their worry, a worry that was so common that I gave it a name—"adulting," meaning how to be an adult. No surprise when Bobbie told me to put a price tag on my idea. We calculated our costs that included chart paper, two easels, a few sets of markers, and hiring a consultant, Jay Klein, to evaluate the program at the end of year one and year two. The total cost for this two-year project was $8,000!

Even though my seven students and their families did not fully understand the adventure they were starting, they eagerly chose to participate because they had trust in me as a teacher.

The results were amazing. Over the next three years the students graduated with jobs; were able to travel independently using public transportation; developed self-advocacy skills; shopped and ate out at restaurants independently. Most of all, family and community members saw the gifts and talents that these previously marginalized young adults possessed. It was so successful that person-centered planning was implemented throughout the school district. That's when it nearly killed me.

Feeling responsible for the project and wanting every child utilizing it to succeed, I made myself available at the convenience of the families. I was exhausted and absent from my family. Managing my teaching responsibilities and facilitating person-centered plans was taking its toll on my mental and physical health. I went to Bobbie suggesting that I reduce my class load so that I could spend my energy on facilitating plans, creating vocational opportunities, and job coaching my students. I began to require students and families to meet with me during school time. But by then, the program and my work had won parents over, and they trusted me implicitly.

Shelley was a co-teacher who attended McGill University with me. She and I tromped the streets of Montreal, having many experiences that brought us closer as friends. After I retired, it was Shelley - who worked at The University of Texas at Austin - who reached out to me to further our work on person-centered planning, creating the Person-Centered Transition Assessment that would later be implemented throughout Texas and considered 'Best Practices.'

Karen, Bobbie, and Shelley influenced and strengthened me through their support and knowledge.

* * *

I have always been a believer in frank, honest conversations with students regarding their disabilities. After an IEP certain accommodations or modifications might be assigned to a student. Accommodations could range from having the student sit in the front row of their classrooms; giving more time for test-taking; working with texts in larger print sizes; listening to audio recordings rather than reading text, etc. Modifications could mean that a student would not be required to learn all the materials in order to pass the class.

Some parents did not appreciate how straightforward I spoke with their children and they would take their complaints to Bobbie. I would take the student aside, help them identify their abilities and giftedness. I would then help them see their barriers to learning and this helped them understand their disABILITY. My goal was to help them understand their eligibility. Cerebral palsy, dyslexia, autism, intellectual developmental disability – in my mind a child should have an awareness of themselves. The more information they had the better they could thrive in the long run. All my efforts as a teacher were to prepare my students for their futures. Even if parents disagreed with the frank conversations I had with their children, it was important that I did my best to draw them in as well. We were all on the same team with the same objectives for the students - a well-rounded life in a community that welcomed and encouraged them to rise to their potential.

Bobbie always supported my efforts in this way and later after she retired I took over her position. Whenever I was in a quandary about how to handle a situation I would ask myself, "What would Bobbie do?" I even got a bracelet made that said "WWBD."

CRAIG

Craig was a junior in high school who mastered German and Spanish and also had straight A's in Science, and Social Studies. He was a whiz in chemistry, and it was his favorite subject. But he struggled in English and using organization skills. He also had difficulty controlling his anger and stress.

Craig's mother knew that I was scheduled to meet with him. She contacted Bobbie asking her to make sure I did not discuss his Autism. Bobbie sided with me and told Craig's mother that he needed to understand. She also assured her that I would be very careful in my conversation with Craig.

I invited his mother to the meeting, but she declined. After

Craig and I discussed his giftedness, he identified that he had a hard time being organized and always felt stressed. We talked about things that helped him and I asked him if he knew anything about Autism. He looked at me with amazement and said "Do I have Autism?" Then he said, "I always thought that 'AU' on my paperwork meant that I was made of gold and that I was the golden boy."

JANETTE

Janette, who had cerebral palsy and did not use words to communicate, was a student of mine at CTC. She had her own version of sign language that was only understood by her family and some staff members. She had such an outgoing personality that we called her a "social butterfly." When she learned that I had a seven-year-old daughter, she told her mother about an idea she had. Why not introduce Mrs. Wilke's daughter to Janette's seven-year-old niece! Thinking this was a lovely idea, we connected the two little girls, who became friends for the rest of their school years.

Lake Highlands High School in Janette's attendance area did not have a program for her level of need. For years her parents requested that Janette attend this school. When I moved from CTC Janette's parents approached the special education director, asking if she could attend my classes. Soon she was in my classroom, where she began using pictures to communicate. I would cut out pictures and put them in a wallet. This was years before the PECS (Picture Exchange Communication System) was developed.

The year before graduating Janette had a job training position at Target in the shoe department. With support, she could use her communication system to ride and pay for public transportation to and from work. Her job at Target was to open boxes of shoes, take out the wrappings, sort the shoes by models and sizes and deliver them to the shoe department.

When Janette was ready to graduate from high school, her parents requested services from the Texas Rehabilitation Services. Although she had shown employment skills, the state deemed Janette unemployable. She was moved to a shelter similar to what she had experienced at CTC. My feelings when I learned of Janette's fate were both anger and determination. I was angry that the state could not comprehend Janette's worth as a human being. Even worse—Janette had experienced what an independent life looked like. Now that she was tucked away each day in some sheltered center, I worried that her beautiful spirit would fade. I had worked so hard with Janette and her family, building up their hopes that she could go into adulthood with a semblance of a future. With her family's hopes dashed, I vowed to never to let this happen again.

It was the summer after Janette graduated that I went to McGill University and learned about Person-Centered Planning. Having this new knowledge gave me a sense of defeat as If I had failed Janette. She was the reason that I instituted Person-Centered Planning. I never wanted to see a student graduate without their potential met.

HENRY

Henry was one of several students from Garland who followed me to Richardson ISD. He was a handsome boy originally from the Philippines. He was also very sensitive and reacted to bullying by getting into fights when other kids called him names such as "retard" or "retardo" or "slow." To Henry, I affirmed that "slow" did not mean "stupid." And to the kids who teased Henry, I told them he was like Heinz Ketchup—that it was so thick and delicious it was worth the wait. From then on, each time someone accused Henry of being slow, he would say, "Yes, but I'm worth the wait."

Because of his learning disability, the Catholic Church had denied Henry the opportunity to have his First Communion. When I heard about this, I knew what to do. I had been teaching religious education or CCD (Confraternity of Christian Doctrine) at St. Patrick's Catholic Church to prepare children to receive the sacraments in their First Communion. Although it was disappointing that the Catholic Church was not as inclusive as it could be, I took it upon myself to take Henry under my wing and prepare him for his first communion.

ETHAN

Ethan was a huge kid. He also had an aggressive, negative type of behavior related to the syndrome he was born with. When it came time to select potential jobs for Ethan, he chose "courtesy clerk". I thought to myself, "What part of courtesy do you think you have?" Ethan insisted that anyone can sack groceries. But I knew this would be a disaster and that he would fail, but he needed the opportunity to try. It is Ethan's right and every child's right to try new ventures and fail at them. 'Dignity of risk' allows a person to have opportunities that are not life-threatening and can help build their self-confidence. Parents of kids with disabilities can be protective to a fault, thereby never employing the useful and necessary 'dignity of risk.'

I arranged for him to participate in Vocational Observation at a local grocery store. This allows a student to observe a job for up to 5 hours and the teacher needs to be present at all times. When a student has the potential to experience a risk while on the job, I set up safety nets. In Ethan's case, I was always present during his observations. The grocery store that I chose was a store where I often shopped. His observation time was the least busy few hours at the store. But I knew it was just a matter of time before Ethan would blow his top. Then it happened.

While Ethan was at the cash register putting groceries into a customer's bags, he put a jug of milk and a carton of bleach into the same bag. The cashier told him that those two items were not to be bagged together. Ethan went ballistic. I had to hurry him outside the store where I could calm him down away from the staring eyes of the customers. I used my most practiced teacher voice, but nothing would settle his anger. I began to feel a tingle of fear down my spine, but when I assured Ethan that he had been helpful, he finally got control of himself. Eventually, I went back into the store to apologize to the customer and the cashier.

Ethan retained his dignity despite his meltdown. He understood that the job as a courtesy clerk was perhaps a wrong choice. Rather than giving up on Ethan and dashing his dreams, I worked with the store manager to find him the perfect job—stocking shelves in the middle of the night, when customers were nowhere in sight.

EVELYN

By the time I met Evelyn, my skills as an educator had grown. With so many students with such a variety of personalities and talents having crossed my path, my instincts had strengthened along with my confidence. But then Evelyn was sent to me, and what I learned from my experience with her would become a turning point for me both professionally and spiritually.

Evelyn arrived in Texas from California. She was born with an intellectual disability that left her unable to verbalize. Her parents had created a system for her to talk through a computer. While I stood facilitating the plan and discussing Evelyn's future, rather than giving her mother any eye contact I concentrated my attention on Evelyn herself. Quickly I had realized that Evelyn's mother was usurping her daughter's control. Evelyn's wants and desires were less important than what her mother felt were priorities.

As my questions were directed at Evelyn, she furiously typed her answers on her computer. Then her mother leaned over to see what she was writing. Before I could react, her mother pulled the plug from Evelyn's computer, making the screen go dark. For a moment I was speechless. All my years of experience and training flew from my mind. The only thing that surfaced was my faith in God. I said to myself, "Lord, what should I do?" While waiting for inspiration, I stood still as if paralyzed in place. Evelyn turned to her mother, expressing how upset she was. Everyone else in the room was also at a loss for words. All the mother did was sit with her head held high and a scowl on her face.

At that moment I surveyed the condition of the room. It was untidy, with objects littering the carpet. Then I noticed a small card resting near my feet. I had just asked the Lord for guidance when my eyes took in the image on the card. The illustration was of a whale, which reminded me of the story of Jonah. When God directed Jonah to preach to people whom Jonah did not trust, God sent a huge storm that endangered the boat Jonah and his men were in. The men tossed Jonah overboard, and the storm disappeared. A whale surfaced and swallowed Jonah, who lived in his belly for three days. When the whale coughed up Jonah onto a beach, Jonah saw that God had saved him. Jonah's faith in God was restored, and he followed the path God had led him to. Jonah went on to successfully preach the word of the Lord, and many people were saved.

Just as Jonah's faith was strengthened, I could feel myself affirming my faith in God. As I stood there I thought, "I started this job for a reason. I was led to this moment." This was a turning point in my life when I knew God had this plan for me. For that reason alone, I knew that an unhappy mother was not going to railroad the good work we were trying to do for her daughter. The meeting continued and ended up being productive. I said to the group, "I think we all need a moment of silence to reflect." After a moment, I plugged in Evelyn's computer and asked her to tell me what she was trying to say.

As for the card with the picture of the whale, I slipped it into my wallet and treasured it for many years. Each time I held it in my hands or caught of glimpse of it in my open wallet, I was reminded of the power of faith.

8

VOCATIONAL TRAINING & ADULTING

The value of work should be offered to anyone willing to take on the tasks of a particular job. For people with disabilities, their work motivation is significantly high. The Texas Education Agency states that a person cannot be deemed unemployable until they are given the opportunity to explore options for training and employment. The potential all of us have as human beings are unlimited. Sometimes our potential just needs to be handled with care and given encouragement. If we can just find our wings, our self-possessed abilities can flourish.

I had been advocating to parents and educators the dignity of risk, the rewards a child can achieve if given the chance to experience failure. To discover the value of work, oftentimes a child or young adult must go through a series of disappointments or failures. This is true for both typical students and those with disabilities. As I've seen time and time again, though, parents of children with disabilities can often be so protective and so bound to the everyday care of their child that the idea of allowing him or her to break free seems impossible.

But in my work, the value of work and the dignity of risk are both critical life experiences that I encouraged parents to allow for their children. And when my students are given these opportunities, that's when I see their wings outspread as they soar into life.

MICHAEL

Michael was a young man who exemplified the notion of the value of work. He had autism as well as an intellectual disability. Everyone in his world said he could not possibly hold down a job. They worried that he did not have the skills or the disposition to be employed. Michael also had the unfortunate habit of taking off running when given the chance. This led people to label him a 'runner.' To discourage the use of this label, I focused on the need to place Michael in situations where safe boundaries were present.

Michael also had a loud, booming voice. Again, acknowledging this definitive trait in Michael told me that we needed to find him a job where his eardrum-popping voice would not be a detriment.

During his person-centered planning meetings, we learned how Michael had taken an interest whenever he saw his dad and his uncle, both veterinarians, wearing scrubs.

As they entered the room, Michael would roar "Doctor!" Michael also loved to visit their animal hospitals where he would be allowed to put on a set of hospital scrubs. We deduced from all this information that Michael had an interest in becoming a doctor. Everyone in his team knew this was not possible, but what job could Michael do capably that would fulfill this dream and meet the qualities of his personality?

At our local hospital, they had a paid job available in the laundry room in the environmental services department. This area of the hospital was very loud with clanging and thrumming machinery. I met with the supervisor and explained the accommodations needed to help Michael succeed in his new job. Michael's job was to fold the towels and washcloths. All the staff surrounding Michael wore scrubs. Michael himself wore a pager so that he knew when his mother had arrived to pick him up.

To support Michael's need for boundaries, his workplace was artfully designed so that he was surrounded by the laundry bin where he pulled the clean towels, and the shelves, where he placed the towels he had folded. He was meticulous about placing the folded towels on the shelf with the tags showing. The nurses loved his work – he made their jobs easier.

There came a time when Michael went away on vacation. While Michael was gone, I received a call from the manager saying that without Michael in the department all the towel folding had been screwed up! None of the tags were showing as they should have been. Michael's high standards were not being followed in his absence. The value of work was so apparent in Michael's case because he himself was of value to his workplace and co-workers.

* * *

Another quality I've noticed in my students getting ready to enter the workplace is determination. No matter the risk or the chance of failure, many of my students would jump right into the job offered to them, no questions asked. The dignity of risk is so effective when people with disabilities are given the chance to try. Even when the person does fail, that failure may offer another new opportunity! These moments will build a person's sense of judgment and teach them that the choices they make can affect their future and their lives.

RICKY

We, humans, are gifted with the ability to communicate with each other to express our needs and emotions. It is so important that we feel understood by our families, friends, and co-workers. For some of my students, their efforts to communicate went unnoticed. Sometimes the techniques they used or the way they adapted their communication methods were met with impatience. It is no wonder that anyone who is feeling misunderstood would lash out and shut down.

Ricky was diagnosed with autism and had a cognitive disability. Most of my students had more significant challenges than Ricky, but his parents wanted him to be in my classroom. If Ricky was criticized, misunderstood, or questioned, he would often lose his temper. I found the best way to communicate with Ricky was to give him extra time to process my words. But there came a day with Ricky when I forgot this strategy. Although it was rough, what we learned is something the two of us share to this day.

Ricky and I were doing a 'community-based instructional lesson.' We had gone to a restaurant so he could learn the skills of ordering food, eating with good table manners, and calculating a tip when paying for his meal. While we were sitting at a table looking at our menus, the server asked Ricky what he would like to order. Ricky gave her a glassy stare and did not respond. I waited a minute then remembered what Ricky had chosen in the past. I said, "Ricky, do you want a cheeseburger?" He continued to stare. I tried again: "Do you want a hamburger with cheese?" He stared. I posed another question: "Do you want something different?" Nothing. Then I asked him, "Do you want pizza?" After that, Ricky threw his menu at me, pushed the table away, and ran. Later, when we returned to school and Ricky had calmed down, I told him that I did not understand what had happened. What he said reminded me that he had a distinct and personal style of communication that I had completely overlooked.

"Your words," he said softly, "are like wax paper." Not grasping his point, I urged him to elaborate. "You asked one question and you didn't give me time to answer. So, it was like you put wax paper over your words. Then you asked another question while I was thinking about the first one. That was another layer of wax paper." Ricky went on to explain that by the time he ran away, I had put five layers of wax paper on my words, making him unable to answer the server's original question.

The next time Ricky caught me off guard, I knew it was a matter of time before he translated his meaning into something I could understand. Ricky had approached me one day and said, "I don't need ExLax." I did not prod him with questions. My patience paid off when he took a breath and refined his point, "I am not irregular, and I need to be in regular education. I don't need special education."

One of Ricky's first jobs was working in the film development department at Target. His primary job was organizing the developed packets of film and putting them in their proper categories. One day an impatient customer asked Ricky to find his photos. When Ricky didn't respond quickly enough, the customer said, "What, are you retarded?" Ricky reacted by pushing over the counter where the film sat, then storming out of the department.

Immediately after we returned to school I sat down with Ricky and asked him what had happened. Ricky, who rarely showed any emotion, looked at me his eyes filled with tears, and said, "If we pray to God can I be normal and not Autistic?" After a moment of silence and a short prayer, I responded, "Ricky, I don't know what God can do so I can't say that God can't make you like everyone else, but I do know that you don't have to act the way that you did, and people don't need to know that you have Autism."

We also came up with a secret signal that I should use to alert him that he was acting 'autistic.' Ricky told me to say, "You are acting the 'A' way." This was our turning point. From then on, Ricky zeroed in on his dream to have his pilot's license and to work on airplanes. He was so determined that I contacted Southwest Airlines and arranged for Ricky to have a summer internship. Although Ricky did not care for the job, he loved being at the airport. After I returned from a vacation, I checked in with Ricky to see how his job was going. Excitedly he said, "You won't believe this! I was flying a plane and buzzed Reunion Tower in downtown Dallas!" I felt my knees go weak, thinking someone had allowed Ricky to get in the cockpit of an airplane and fly. But I soon realized someone had allowed Ricky to practice flying in the flight simulator!

After his summer job at the airport ended, I re-evaluated his skillset and found him a job at Jiffy Lube. He never missed a day on the job, but he was not satisfied. He longed to be in or near airplanes. Then the ideal job presented itself. Ricky was hired to clean private airplanes at Addison Airport. He was well paid and delighted in his job. But when the company he worked for went out of business, Ricky became unemployed for a short time then got a job working at a car rental business close to the airport.

His dream and passion for flying airplanes has never diminished. Today he is working towards getting his pilot's license. He even figured out how to use a Groupon, getting two lessons at half price!

It has been 30 years since Ricky was a boy in my classroom. Over this time, he and I together have done trainings for school districts, churches, educational service centers, and businesses. Working so closely over the years has meant that from time to time I have had to use our secret signal, always said with a smile: "You are acting the 'A' way!"

MATTHEW

Matthew was another student whose parents insisted that he be placed in my classroom. He and Ricky were classmates, and just as I assisted Ricky with his vocational opportunities, Matthew's parents hoped I could do the same for him.

Matthew's brain worked differently than the 'ordinary' students. He was a renowned whiz at math. In fact, we could not allow Matthew to take math quizzes and tests in his general education classroom because too many other students would cheat by looking at his paper. If Matthew looked at a number just one time, such as a phone number or social security number, he would store it in his memory bank forever. If you said to him the date of any year, he could tell you the day of the week that date fell on.

One day while I was spot-checking Matthew at his job as a cashier at a Target Department store, a customer wrote a check. Matthew remembered the person's driver's license number from a previous visit. Another time Matthew must have been within earshot when I was arranging my annual car inspection. Because a year later Matthew reminded me that it was time to have my car checked.

There came a day when I picked up my phone, and it was Matthew. The day had been particularly stressful for me. My husband, Dave, was diagnosed with cancer earlier that day. I was honest with Matthew and told him this was a bad time for me to talk. Then I told him about Dave's condition. Matthew got very upset on the other end of the line, worrying that Dave was going to die. I said to him, "No, Matthew, he's not going to die." Matthew thought about it for a moment, then said, "OK, tell him to check his inspection sticker."

Matthew was hired by our local hospital to work in the phlebotomy laboratory. A common trait of Matthews's was to mumble affirmations to himself. This both calmed and motivated him. One day, while he walked down a hospital hallway during his daily shift, he noticed people staring at him. He realized he must have been saying his affirmations and that the people around him were wondering what he was talking about. He knew he needed to come up with a solution so that he would not be misunderstood. And when he did, he told me his plan. "Debbie," he said, "if anyone asks what I am saying, I am going to just tell them that I am praying." Twenty-four years later, Matthew is still working in this job.

DANNY

I believe that when you open your ears and listen with your heart, solutions will come to you. This is what I try to do with all my students. For a student of mine named Danny, this approach made all the difference. I've seen how having a job can change the way a person lives their life. One day they behave a certain way, and the next, because of the work they are doing, everything changes. This is exactly what happened to Danny.

Danny was not my favorite student. This was most likely because he refused to bathe. My aversion to Danny had more to do with the smell he emitted rather than who he was as a person. Danny was born with Down Syndrome. He was incredibly smart. His parents tried relentlessly to convince him to take a daily shower but to no avail.

As for his vocational training, each time I found a job for him, he would end up getting fired. Was it because of his body odor? Then it hit me. I needed to find him a job where taking a bath was low on the priority list of qualifications. A local recycling plant had an opening, and I jumped on it for Danny. After his third month working at the plant, he came to see me. He said, "Ms. Wilkes, I hate my job." When I asked him why, he said, "Because it stinks!" After that job experience, Danny changed his life and his opportunities. He began to regularly bathe. This act alone widened his circle of opportunities.

9

INTERDEPENDENCE

As a body is one, though it has many parts, and all the parts of the body, though many, are one body so also Christ. If one part suffers, all the parts suffer with it; if one part is honored, all the parts share its joy.

-First Letter to the Corinthians

Looking back over my career these past 49 years, I know that being a teacher has never been a job to me. It is an avocation. Even if a paycheck was not part of the deal, teaching and counseling people with disabilities of all ages would have been my daily work. Over time I have learned how my faith in God is tied to the work I do. I believe that God does not make mistakes. The hundreds of people who I have served are all miracles and are all perfect in God's eyes. There is nothing wrong with them. We are all made in God's likeness. He made each of us different. The more we recognize the giftedness that each and every one of us brings, the more we understand our Savior. He made us the way we were supposed to be made.

But this world throws up challenges that are obvious to some and confusing to others. To navigate life as we enter adulthood requires support, motivation, and pinpointing our passions. Having a helping hand, someone who can offer understanding and provide support is where I come in. One of my goals in preparing young people to enter the world of 'adulting' is to give them confidence that they can self-advocate. For some of them, their parents have done all the heavy lifting. But when they go to bat for themselves, I can see the pride in their faces and bodies. Confidence comes with independence. This does not mean we abandon our support systems. In fact, none of us are fully independent.

Kathie Snow, an author and public speaker who has become an expert in the field of raising successful children with disabilities, expanded on the term 'interdependence.' She writes that our children, as well as we ourselves, are interdependent, meaning we rely on others to assist us beyond just walking and talking. When we isolate our children from other social or interactive opportunities because we need to be in charge, OR when we insist that they be independent and fend for themselves, they can feel lonely and left out. But when they rely on technology, relationships, and service providers, they are acting interdependently. This allows for inclusion in ordinary life as well as giving them a chance to help others.

Today I facilitate a self-determination and self-advocacy

group for young adults who have completed their person-centered plan. They have assessed what their passions are, and we have mapped out possible jobs and careers living opportunities, and recreational options. Next, we find jobs, places to live, or places to hang out that suit their skills. In September 2020 two of the group members, Logan and Joe were guests on a panel hosted by Highland Park United Methodist Church. They both expressed themselves beautifully, detailing their work lives and examples of how they have determined their lives and advocated for themselves while helping each other.

LOGAN

Logan is a 30-year-old young woman who was diagnosed with autism at the age of 26. After completing her person-centered plan, we determined that art, photography, and dogs were her passions. Three years ago, Logan was hired to bathe the dogs in a dog grooming business. But getting to this moment was not an easy road. Through unfortunate experiences, Logan has become highly proficient at self-advocacy.

While in dog grooming school, Logan dealt with bullying. One day while trimming a dog's fur, an instructor came up to her, looked at the cut, and called Logan an "idiot." The comment made Logan feel her motivation drain from her body. When Logan told me what had happened I helped her to go to the manager and explain that she does best when she can observe an action several times. She asked the manager to repeat the grooming techniques over and over. The manager obliged, and Logan soon graduated from dog grooming school.

But recently, while working in a dog grooming shop, Logan again experienced bullying. Because Logan trusted the owner of the shop, she was able to tell her, "I was being bullied by that groomer." She switched me to another groomer who was nicer to me and could see my talent and how good a bather I am."

My goal is to work my way out of a job and allow the person to soar without my help. I was proud that Logan felt confident enough not to contact me about her problem. She and her boss took a long walk to discuss Logan's feelings, and it was clear she was well understood. I've noticed that sometimes when other people in our group reach out to Logan for advice or ideas, Logan's texts back to them are exactly what I would have said! Sometimes, reading her texts, it's like I'm reading my own words!

Prescription medications are commonly needed by children with disabilities. In Logan's case, she noticed that her medications were the cause of her sleeplessness. She felt drowsy at work, and it was impacting her quality of life. Her parents preferred that she remain on the medications. But again, Logan advocated for herself and got off the prescription medications. A few days into being prescription drug-free, Logan says, "Even my boss noticed how much happier I was."

JOE

At the age of six, Joe was diagnosed with autism. Today Joe believes that kids with disabilities are perfect. He says, "There is nothing to fix." But this did not stop his school years from being filled with often insurmountable obstacles and heartache. The bullying in elementary school was constant. Then when he was nine years old, Joe took a piano lesson that changed his life. Regarding the elderly woman who was his piano teacher, Joe says, "I owe that lady everything." Joe can play almost any tune by ear—although he can also read music. Kids took a new look at Joe when they heard him play. Suddenly he had a cool factor.

On September 11th, 2001, Joe was a freshman in high school. Seeing the images of the attack on the World Trade Center in New York City and the Pentagon in Washington DC horrified Joe. Afterward, he suffered from post-traumatic stress syndrome (PTSD). His minds-eye could not erase the brutality that he witnessed that day.

One time while working at a movie theater, Joe went into a darkened theater to do a headcount. The sounds and images on the screen triggered his PTSD. Joe ran out of the theater crying. He lashed out at a fellow employee, then apologized. He told his manager and asked that he no longer be required to step into theaters where movies were playing. His manager listened to Joe's concerns and changed Joe's job description. One day Joe talked to a musician friend of his, telling her how his PTSD was affecting his job. She told Joe to write it all down. The writing was like therapy. The result was a poem titled "Looking at the Sky."

As a musician, Joe has impressive accomplishments. After graduating with degrees in recording technology, music performance, and composition/arrangement of digital music, Joe is now a professional musician. He is in two bands and composed the arrangements for a steel drum ensemble at Richland College. But whereas music is an area in which Joe shows great proficiency, humor, and sarcasm expressed by others can go right over his head. Joe says, "I take stuff way too literally. People don't get it, so I have to tell them I am in the dark. I have a sense of humor, but sometimes I don't pick up on other people's jokes. When it comes to catching on to sarcasm, I am a sleepy slug."

Looking at the Sky
By Joe Sanchez

Now you know the Reaper was summoned here that day
And you know he took so many innocent lives away
To recall my ordeals from the past, I now decide
No, I can't run away, I've nowhere to hide

When near 3,000 people were smoked like cheap cigars,
I could be either a sweet turtle dove or an exploding Death Star
Consistently fighting a losing battle within
Though I was never a vet, I may as well have been

Upon hearing, I thought it was a lie
Then I saw the vid, looking at the sky
At once consumed by fires of revenge
While playing drums in the high school band

And now I tried to find a way to hurt the ones that hurt me,
Barely caring if anyone would assist or desert me
As time ticked slowly by, things got progressively more adverse
There was some good, but the bad kept getting worse and worse

Music was still there, but it was little consolation
Whenever I'd get to feeling better, it was still constant regression
Almost always grim defeat, and to this day, I wonder why
I would get so desperate to think, 'Why even try?'

After a few months, I could think of nothing else
Though many other ways were tried, nothing seemed to help
I made a few attempts, and all were epic fails,
But progress was still crawling slower than a sleepy snail

Sent away to sort out my head,
Where I eventually realized I was going to wind up

confined or dead
Set free to rejoin my blood band
Yet from here on out, I'll never understand

10

PERSONAL TRANSITIONING

Just as transitioning happens for my students, I too was experiencing transitioning in my life. In 1995, my husband Dave was diagnosed with cancer. Not only was this a difficult time emotionally for our family, but we were also experiencing financial stress. During these years my own strength and self-determination would be put on trial. Rather than suffering alone and shouldering all my burdens, I would reach out for help. Figuring out that I could rely on others—therapists, spiritual guides, and my family—made it possible for me to survive and remain healthy.

Before Dave's diagnosis, he became verbally abusive towards me. His hostility and anger were making it difficult for me to be near him. We knew he was sick, but the diagnosis had not yet been made. His fear of the unknown was wreaking havoc on our lives. Then the week before his appointment for a scan that would answer our questions, I called my sisters Janet and Merdi, and asked if they could meet me for lunch. At the restaurant, I told them how emotionally abusive Dave had become. I said out loud that I could no longer live like this and that I might consider getting a divorce. Being a devout Catholic where divorce is not an option, my sisters immediately understood the depths of my despair.

I accompanied Dave to his scan appointment. The young radiologist who reviewed Dave's results walked into the room where we were waiting. He said, "Oh wow, I guess you don't have long to live." I was floored by his callous remark. Devastated, Dave and I went home. We sat in our den and really looked at each other. We were facing his death which meant everything had to change. I told him about my lunch conversation with my sisters. How his abusive treatment of me had to stop. How I was this close to asking for a divorce. Dave began to cry, then we were weeping together. We made new vows of support, love, and commitment. From that day on, whenever Dave lashed out at me, I would quickly remind him of those vows, and he would apologize. Our marriage had come back from the brink. Until the day he died many years later, Dave and I stayed true to each other rediscovering the joy and strength in our relationship.

* * *

One day the director of special education called me into her office. Thinking a parent had complained about me, I gathered my papers ready to defend myself. But once I had seated myself across from Bobbie and her boos, they told me to put away my papers. Bobbie opened by saying she wanted to talk to me about transitioning my job. They needed me to oversee the vocational programs as the administrator. I loved being a teacher, and alarm bells were going off in my head that I could soon find myself in a job that I hated. I pointed out that I did not have the proper certification. Not to worry, I was told. I could take over the job immediately and get the certification over the summer. In fact, I was given an ultimatum. In what I hoped was a joking manner, they flat out said that if I decided to not take this job, then I could leave to find something else.

I ended up getting the certification and taking the job as an administrator overseeing vocational education and transition. I was soon making more money but also working longer hours. Years later I would realize that this job was the perfect stepping stone for the consulting business I would open one day. The money was important too, as my girls were approaching their college years.

Bobbie began referring me and the person-centered planning proces to other colleagues in different school districts. She pointed out that no one else was doing this type of planning. At first, some parents pushed back. Why would they invest time and emotional energy into something that was so rare? But Vicki Templeton and I had designed the program and we wanted to share it beyond our own district's borders. I will never forget the first training we did for a service center in Corpus Christi. They paid us $100 each for the full day! I was floored! Could this area of expertise that I had be of value? Could Vicki and I someday start a consulting business? We came up with a plan: We could set up an employment program using person-centered planning and apply for funding through the Texas Rehabilitation Commission. But our excitement was short-lived. Vicki fell ill and I knew, with my family life in disarray, I could not do this alone. But rather than locking these ideas into a vault never to be heard from again, I decided to just set them on a shelf where I could take them down one day and reconsider the possibilities.

Even in my job at school, the popularity of person-centered planning was building. Parents were more frequently requesting it for their kids. It was my job to fulfill these requests. Although I was not being paid specifically for this service, I didn't care. What the demand showed me was that the program was working. As I completed plan after plan, helping student after student, my abilities and intuition strengthened. I trained the teachers in the Transition Program to facilitate the process and even more students were served. If I had a crystal ball, I have no doubt it would show me in my future days doing private person-centered planning from within the homes of my clients, with no school classrooms or conference rooms in sight.

A young woman named Stacy was enrolled in my class at Lake Highlands. Not only did she have spina bifida, but she also had a severe case of SRK – Spoiled Rotten Kid. Stacy was in a wheelchair. But she refused to use her own muscle power to move her chair. So rather than argue with her, someone in her family always came along to push her chair wherever she needed to go. I knew all this enabling would not bring Stacy the independence she should be striving for. So, one day I taped a sign to the back of her wheelchair that read, "Please don't push me. I can do it myself." The clever girl one-upped me by backing up her wheelchair (using her own muscle-power) to a wall where no one could read the sign.

Stacy's determination was evident. I too had increasing determination to find her a job. Stacy needed to be catheterized, so I needed to find an employer who could provide this for her while she was on the job. I made a cold call to Presbyterian Hospital in Dallas. Admittedly when I said that I was from Lake Highlands High School vocational programs I did not disclose that I work with students with disabilities. The operator sent my call to Human Resources, and I spoke with a woman named Jan. As I described Stacy as a possible candidate for employment at the hospital, I could feel Jan pulling back. In my heart, I just knew this hospital was where Stacy belonged. Just then I could feel God's presence. His strength engulfed me and the words I needed to convince Jan suddenly came clear. I told her, "I think you owe Stacy an opportunity." Jan was taken aback by my bluntness. I continued, "Stacy was born in this hospital. She was in the NICU where your staff kept her alive. Maybe the doctors and nurses felt wonderful that they kept her alive, but here she is today ready to give back."

To my shock, Jan started to cry. She said, "I was working in the NICU about the time when Stacy was born. I may have known her." I gently said, "When she was a newborn, you and the staff knew she had value. You worked to save her." Within weeks, Stacy was hired. In the coming years, Presbyterian Hospital hired several of our other students.

My persistence gave me courage. Over the next months, I was able to convince Burger King, Wendy's, and a local hobby shop to hire kids in our program. Something few school staff did was tap into the parents' resources. Everyone remained on their sidelines. Parents did not see a deliberate role for themselves in finding their children work. I had no hesitation in asking parents to give me leads of people they knew who could possibly hire our students. Many of them did. My cold calls felt a bit warmer as I could drop the name of the parents, someone the employer knew.

* * *

Dave was diagnosed with two types of cancer and his medical bills were becoming astronomical. Dave had a Cobra policy but my insurance would not pay for any pre-existing conditions and everything was pre-existing for Dave. We were desperate to do whatever it took to beat the cancer. Dave entered several drug therapy trials, each one a new hope for a cure. I was unaware of how entrenched in stress I had become. I thought my job was giving me strength. But co-workers would tell me to take a leave of absence.

They assumed that the daily trials inside a special education program were adding to my stress. What they did not understand was that my work was the only thing I could control. But was this true?

The feelings of being overwhelmed and unfocused persisted. Although my faith in God was a saving grace, I knew I needed to talk to someone. I found a therapist and was soon diagnosed with situational clinical depression. Although I refused any prescriptions for medication, I felt that the sessions with the therapist were beginning to help me.

Despite the expense, Dave and I took a trip to England and Ireland. With my sister Merdi and her husband, we visited our sister Janet and her husband who were living in London. Then toured the country where my favorite authors once lived. Dublin took us to the locations where Maeve Binchy wrote her novels and we toured Thomas Hardy's Wessex. In the south of England, we were able to discover the cliffs and seashore where Rosamunde Pilcher set her characters and stories.

But even though visiting these foreign lands felt refreshing, I could not shake the uneasy feelings stemming from our daily struggles back in Texas. One day as I walked through a field overlooking the waters of the English Channel, painful thoughts filled my head. "No one likes you! No one wants to be with you! You are worthless!" I breathed deep the ocean air and realized these thoughts were manifesting my depression. When we returned home, I asked my therapist to refer me to a psychiatrist. I could no longer do this on my own. I was ready for a prescription.

But my sister Janet was also someone I could lean on. In February 1997 Dave's cancer was taking its toll and I had to have surgery on my neck. My daughter Jamille, a senior in high school, was practically bouncing off the walls with all her end-of-school activities. Our finances were stretched to the limit, and I could feel the end of my rope getting close. One day at church, with my neck in a brace, Janet came up to me and put her arms around my shoulders. She could just see the weight of the world etched on my face. She remembers me telling her, "I don't know how I can keep doing this." Janet may not have had the silver lining to make my life all better, but her ability to simply listen to me, just like when we were kids, gave me strength.

My psychiatrist was wonderful. She prescribed Wellbutrin, which I remained on for five years. Sessions with her were transformative. She and I were both dealing with aging mothers. One time she said to me, "I should be paying you for these sessions!"

To this day I am a strong advocate for therapy and counseling. God invented these resources to support us. We are strong when we understand that we are weak. Having a mental illness is not something we should hide or label as bad. Our brains may be suffering a chemical imbalance, which is something that can be addressed and treated.

* * *

Since the day He revealed Himself to me and Father Schott, I have continued to feel close to the Holy Spirit. I feel so lucky that He has remained nearby. But I will never forget another time when the Holy Spirit cascaded His presence over Dave and me.

Early in Dave's diagnosis, the nurses were preparing for the surgeon to remove Dave's kidney due to renal carcinoma. The mood was pessimistic, and the doctors told us the procedure was potentially dangerous. As Dave laid on the gurney and we held hands before he was to be moved into the operating room, I suddenly felt a tingle and knew without question that the Holy Spirit was surrounding us. I said, "Dave, do you feel something around you?" He looked at me and said, "Yeah, I feel like there's this cocoon all around me, hugging us, both of us." I said, "That's the Holy Spirit."

I do not consider myself an evangelist, but I do pray for the Holy Spirit to appear. He arrives at times of confusion or when a serious question hangs in the balance. On the morning of his surgery, Dave described the feeling of the Holy Spirit's presence beautifully.

Dave lived another 11 years. Then in 2007, as we were in bed lying side by side, with our girls, son-in-law, and future son-in-law in the room, Dave raised his arms as if being lifted up and then he passed away.

LEVI

When Levi was in the seventh grade, I did his person-centered plan. He was born with cerebral palsy and an intellectual disability, and he was mostly confined to his wheelchair. I was encouraged to see that Levi was really beginning to practice his self-advocacy skills. This became especially apparent when one day his mother, a school nurse, called me to ask if I could attend Levi's IEP meeting. She said, "He won't get out of his wheelchair during his PE class." I told her that this did not sound like the Levi we knew.

I made my way to the room where Levi was waiting for me. The school staff had decided to complete a functional behavior analysis (FBA) to figure out why Levi was insistent that he remain in his wheelchair. An FBA identifies the cause of the problem behaviors, then indicates ways in which to mitigate or eliminate the behaviors. During the IEP meeting, the behavior specialist explained the assessment. Levi looked at me and spoke. His speech was very slow, and he drew out his consonants, making the listener pay close attention. I knew if he were given the patience to express himself, perhaps he could simply explain the problem.

"Mrs. Wilkes," he said very carefully, "My father said I was not supposed to get out of this chair." I pondered this, knowing full well that Levi's father would want his son to participate in PE class. When Levi's mother learned of his reasoning, she said, "Oh! His dad has been working on our back deck and told Levi to remain in his chair for safety!" I could see then how Levi took his father's instructions to mean the wheelchair was where he was supposed to be 24/7. The school did not need to waste time and resources to conduct an FBA, they only had to talk to Levi!

While I secretly applauded Levi for sticking to his guns and advocating for himself, I also thought that if children with similar speech patterns were provided with some patience and time, they would be understood. For students with speech differences, we need to slow the world down and offer encouragement. We can also suggest that they explain their point in a different way. We should practice empathy by putting our feet into their shoes so that we can interpret their meaning. Because seeing a child's face as they register that you understood them is a wonderful gift.

JESSICA

Jessica's mother contacted me when Jessica was in 5th grade. She had heard about my work and she wanted to make sure that her daughter had the benefit of transition planning at an early age without losing any opportunities. She had cerebral palsy used a wheelchair and had cortical blindness. Later when I met Jessica, I knew she was a beautiful force to be reckoned with. Her tenacity was infectious. She had a paraprofessional who helped her in general education classes, but in reality, this person was doing all of her work. Jessica didn't believe this and thought that she was earning her grades on her own. She insisted on taking the state assessment tests with only the accommodation of someone reading to her and writing what was dictated. Her mother agreed.

The three days of testing seemed endless. Jessica was traumatized as were her parents and me! We were in agreement that she complete the tests knowing that she would fail. Her parents, Betty and Rick understood the concept of taking risks - the Dignity of Risk - letting their daughter fail and allowing her to self-actualize.

I remained in Jessica's life as she grew into adulthood. While I was working in the Transition Program I had received a grant from the Developmental Disabilities of Texas to create an employment skills class that would be taught at the community college. Jessica was one of the first students to complete the class and due to her energy, charisma, and intelligence, I hired Jessica to co-teach the class.

Jessica has been working at the regional educational services office. She has limited mobility in her upper body such that reaching across the desktop to use an electric stapler and hole punch was difficult. Numerous consultants were brought in to rectify the problem such as occupational and physical therapists. When a solution had not been found, Jessica turned to me and said, "Don't you think if they would just put risers underneath my chair, it would give me the height I need to do it all?" Jessica had figured it out. When the risers were put into place, her problem was solved.

NORA

Finding employment for Nora proved to be all about listening. Along with an intellectual disability, Nora had many talents. She loved to read, was a fashionable dresser, and was a wonderful communicator. While considering possible jobs for her, we thought working in a bank where she could put receipts in order might be fulfilling. But after working at the bank for a few weeks, Nora let us know this was not the job for her. "What about working in a library?" I asked. She turned down that idea too.

Recently my grandfather had passed away, so I had spent time at our local funeral home. There I made a personal connection with the funeral director by giving him a copy of the book on railroads that my grandfather had written. It occurred to me that perhaps this environment might be a workplace Nora could thrive in because Nora had absences due to going to funerals and seemed to be interested in this area. I set up an appointment with the funeral director. Although he was supportive of people with disabilities being employed, he was doubtful that Nora could handle the workload. I suggested that he allow Nora to practice her interviewing skills with him. He agreed, and the interview was scheduled.

Nora promptly arrived at her interview appointment dressed in a dark suit, with her hair styled and her make-up beautifully applied. The funeral director asked her many questions, all of which she answered perfectly. He missed the most important question— "Why do you want to work for a funeral home?" Instead, he said, "Do you have any questions for me?" With that, Nora peppered him with well-thought-out questions:

"Why do you use different color embalming fluids?"

"Do bones need to be broken to put on the clothing?"

"Are there special stylists that come to do the person's hair and make-up? If so, what sort of training do they need?"

The funeral director was amazed and impressed with Nora's interest. We stood up, and he thanked us for coming in. After we had left, and before I had even had a chance to follow up with a phone call, he called me. He said that he recognized Nora's zeal for the position and had decided to give her a chance. Nora was hired!

She loved the job. Her tasks were to set up the viewing rooms by strategically placing vases of flowers and making sure there were carafes of water and boxes of tissue. She also managed the guest sign-in books. After a service ended, Nora would clean the viewing room, getting it ready for the next service. Her boss, the funeral director, checked in with her after each shift. He reported to me that I did not need to monitor Nora. Her work was meticulous, and she was an excellent employee.

11

JOSÉ

I n 1996 I met a young man named José who had autism. He was only 18, but during the time that I worked with José, he would reveal to me many valuable pieces of wisdom that I continue to use today.

José's family came to the US illegally. When amnesty was offered to illegal immigrants, his family was able to register for documentation. But they did not register José. Why? I can't be sure, but perhaps they never imagined that José could ever hold down a job or need citizenship.

José was not able to verbalize. To express himself he often resorted to aggression and violence. One time, to express his anger, he broke a teacher's collarbone. Despite these formidable qualities, José had the right to a public education, so he came into my program. One of the first things I taught him was how to use pictures to communicate. The card that said "STOP" was very useful for José. When he held it up, it was often during moments where he might otherwise have lost his cool.

José loved to be outside. He also enjoyed riding in buses. But his favorite activity was to have something in his hands that he could flip back and forth. If he didn't have a "flippy" in his hand he would search for one and his imagination knew no bounds. One day as we were walking in the neighborhood, he spied the rubber seal around the windshield and determined that this would be his next target. There was no stopping him! He took the seal and used it as his "flippy." I left a note on the car window telling the owner to contact me. Once again Bobbie had to make a request of the budget department to pay for a windshield rubber seal. My boss, looking at my expense report, used to laugh at me and say, "Every month I sure enjoy seeing what strange objects you end up buying for José."

I needed to be creative to find a way for José' to earn money even though he was an undocumented worker. A friend of mine suggested I contact a local real estate agency. They needed someone to take stacks of flyers and hang them throughout the neighborhood. José was perfect for the job—he loved the long walks outdoors, and he was paid by the realtor for each door hanger he put into place. I was now able to take him shopping where he could use the money he had earned to purchase new inner tubes that would serve as his flippy's.

One day while I was accompanying José hanging real estate flyers, we entered an upscale neighborhood. Nearby there was a house with the front door wide open. Inside we could see that they were setting up for a tea party. Before I could react, José dashed up the walkway and into the house. He began to help himself to a glass of lemonade and a handful of cookies. Luckily the ladies of the house were completely understanding. This helped me to understand that with José, I would receive little warning when he was about to react to something. And sometimes this was to my detriment.

I taught José how to use public transportation. Although he had learned how to ride buses, on this day I waited with him at the bus stop. Then it started to rain. Like lightning, José became enraged. He leaned into my face and bit me on the cheek! I knew this was a transformative moment. I did not react. I said to myself, "This is a God moment, and you just need to figure this out." What occurred to me was one word—chaos. We were facing an event (rain) that was out of our control. Later I introduced him to a card called Chaos. I had to teach him that chaos would happen but that we could get through it and put the chaos behind us. To do this, I decided to create controlled chaos.

At a local recreation center, I arranged for José to enjoy one of his preferred activities. When we got to the center, the activity was unavailable. I flashed the Chaos card in front of his eyes. His reaction? He swung his arm as if to hit me. Then he let it drop to his side. He understood that the chaos would not last and that soon it would be over.

I never knew what José's cognitive ability was. But I

became convinced that his understanding of language and the world around him was profound. One day, my boss came to observe me in the community where I was teaching. I knew that with José, it was best to talk less rather than more. But on that day my nervousness was making me talk too much. Within minutes, José held up his "STOP" card. I was elated. He was using his tools. Chaos was prevented.

Routines helped José to thrive. As part of his educational program, he would use district money to buy his breakfast at a nearby McDonald's. José would take his breakfast consisting of pancakes, sausage, hash browns, and milk to a table, then reach into his backpack and pull out a flippy object. His patronage was so frequent and expected that soon everyone at the restaurant came to know and accept José. People would give him friendly hellos even though José mostly ignored them. One year at Christmas, while I was having breakfast with José, one of the regular patrons came to our table and gave José a Christmas present. He opened the gift to discover that it was a flippy. I started to cry.

How lovely that José, despite his disability and his inability to interact with people in the restaurant, was accepted as part of the community. His frequent visits to the restaurant created a sort of friendship. He spent his money there and enjoyed the food. Seeing him respected like that still brings tears to my eyes. This is an example that friendship is created by proximity and frequency of seeing people.

Ultimately, I was able to get legal status for José through a friend of mine who worked at Region 1 Educational Services in Laredo. Next, with a Spanish-speaking interpreter, I set up a meeting with José and his parents to complete his person-centered plan. Shortly after that, José and his family moved away. I may never know the outcome of José's life, but when I think of him, I am so grateful to him for helping me to discover that the community can display acceptance and friendship to those who appear different than them.

12

CLOSE TO HOME

"Christ has no body not, but yours. No hands, no feet on earth, but yours. Yours are the eyes through which Christ looks compassion into the world. Yours are the feet with which Christ walks to do good. Yours are the hands with which Christ blesses the world."

- Teresa of Avila

In February of 2007, my husband Dave passed away. My daughters were heartbroken, yet Jamille stepped in and helped with all the details of dealing with death. She helped me with Social Security, changing bank accounts, and any other necessary tasks. My sisters knew how I was hurting and planned a trip to Maine and Nova Scotia for the summer after Dave's death. But I still felt a deep loneliness.

I couldn't continue to burden my daughters with my feelings. My childhood best friend, Terri, was instrumental in giving me comfort and support. Years before, she and her husband had moved to Fort Worth, Texas, just 45 minutes away from my home. Terri married a doctor who specialized in nephrology, the area of kidney disease. When Dave was sick with cancer, Terri's husband, Charlie, helped us negotiate the paths for his care. During each of Dave's surgeries, Terri was by my side in the hospital waiting room. With Dave gone, Terri let me rest my head on her shoulder as she understood my profound loneliness.

During our last Christmas together Dave had given me a ring that he had designed. It was a band with three diamonds in a row. He told me, "They represent the past, present, and your future. I want you to be happy and I want you to move on. I really want you to get married again." A year after he died, I removed my wedding band and replaced it with this beautiful ring that had layers of meaning. After three years I was able to discard the antidepressant medication. I felt the work I had done with my counselor was complete. It was 2010 and my body and mind felt healthy and ready to explore that third diamond in my ring – the future. As if Dave's dying wishes were coming true, three years later I met the man who would become my second husband.

My daughters, Beth and Jamille, were relieved and excited to see me come back to life. Jamille suggested that I create a profile on a dating website. First, I signed up on a Catholic dating site. It proved to be terrible! It felt clunky and invasive and not a single person on it appealed to me. Next, I found a website called Great Expectations. Because it was expensive to join, the people I met would be professional and hopefully more interesting and compatible. I was matched with a counselor who conducted an interview with me. I uploaded professional photos and soon my profile was ready for action.

That Christmas, three years after Dave died, I met another David. Our first date was a disaster. He had picked out a restaurant and we agreed on the time to meet. Despite the butterflies having a heyday in my stomach, I got myself ready and arrived right on time. I waited and waited, but the guy never showed up! He called my cellphone wondering where I was. It turned out the restaurant had several locations, and I was at the wrong one.

Later the evening, we did have our first "encounter" at a restaurant that was close to my home – no chance for a mix-up. Afterward, as we were getting up to leave, David said to me, "You are going to meet someone who will blow your socks off." I took that to mean that he did not think he was that guy for me. While I actually enjoyed our meeting, I realized that he didn't have a suitable profile for me. He was divorced, not Catholic, and worked in a business that sounded shady.

David pursued me gently. He was so patient, giving me a wide berth to just get used to the idea of having a new man in my life. Even after four months of seeing him regularly, I did not feel able to confide in anyone about him. Was it because he had been married and divorced? Perhaps because he was not Catholic? Would his business of selling used cars look questionable to some folks? Whatever the reasons for keeping David away from my loved ones, this would eventually prove to be a big mistake. But I so enjoyed his company, and our relationship was progressing. Hiding him from my children and friends felt dishonest. Especially when at work my colleagues started guessing that I was seeing someone. I just acted casual and said, "Yeah, but he's just practice."

Around our six-month anniversary of dating, David finally met my friends and family. I was retiring from my job and invited him to my retirement party. When it became clear to my daughters how long I had been with David without their knowledge, they took the news hard. How could their mother who had taught them values and morals seriously date a man they knew nothing about?

Soon after, David and I planned to go on a trip together to the Big Bend National Park in the south tip of Texas. I knew I had to come clean with the five dearest people in my life: my two daughters, my two sisters, and my mother. How could they accept this man who I was going to spend a weekend with if they did not understand my deep feelings for him? I was prepared for the worst. Instead, I got a mixed bag. My mother said, "That's the only way you're going to get to know him. You need to do it and I can tell you're happy, you're the person you used to be before Dave got sick." My sisters reacted with so much excitement that they gave me the courage I needed to tell my daughters.

The person I had become during the past year reminded

me of the person I was in the early years of my marriage with Dave. Just as I was then, now I was happy, motivated and hopeful for the future. But my girls were unsure if they could trust this person who was still their mother. She was doing things that were the opposite of what she had taught them.

My daughters were determined to not accept David. There was a time when one of my girls and her husband turned their backs on David when he approached them at a social gathering. I chalked this up to them not knowing who he was as a person and the mistakes I made in introducing him to my life. To them, he was a caricature of someone outside of their comfort zone.

Eight years after meeting David when my daughter Beth and her family moved within a mile of my house, we had more opportunities to spend time together. And like a miracle as soon as they got to know the real David, the walls began to fall away. I could not help but compare this to the misconceptions people have about those who are disabled. When seeing someone in a wheelchair we develop a one-dimensional image of that person. We may have preconceived notions that make us fearful. But once you allow that person to get a foot in the door, where you come to appreciate their humanity, acceptance, and friendship can move in.

During the first three years of dating, David proposed to me several times. Each time I turned him down. I longed for my daughters to understand how happy he made me. It was not that I needed their approval, but I could not allow a rift to form between me and my girls. I wanted them to observe how David honored and respected my family and their father. He always had a ready ear to hear stories about Dave Wilkes. He was so supportive that a family portrait of Dave, my girls with their husbands, and me hung in a place of prominence in my house.

I wanted my girls to see first-hand how David kept me from getting too serious. He brought out my laughter and made me smile all the time. Even though he himself was not a follower of Christ, his support of that area of my life was profound. He may not believe in God, but he completely believed in me.

This is why when he and I were on a trip to Lake Tahoe, California, I finally agreed to marry him. It was a bitterly cold October afternoon at Lassen Volcanic National Park. And there in front of me was the kindest man who wanted to make me his wife. I said, "If you want to ask me to marry you again, you can." David's face lit up and he popped the question. Of course, I said yes.

Not being prepared for this moment, David did not have a ring handy. My precious three diamond ring was on my left hand right where an engagement ring belonged. David could see my face fall when he suggested we go ring shopping. He could see how important it was for me to wear Dave's ring. His solution melted my heart and confirmed why I loved him. We had two rings designed – one an engagement ring and the other a wedding ring. These two new rings would live on each side of the ring Dave had made.

* * *

Marriage to David and having more time due to not working for the school district opened the world to me. He was a huge history buff and he loved nothing more than to visit historical sites in the US. Because he was born and raised in Chicago, most of his travels in the past years had taken him west of the Mississippi River. I was raised on the East coast so most of my experiences on the road were east of the Mississippi. This meant that we could introduce each other to new vistas through our perspective lenses.

With Covid, we don't feel comfortable getting on an airplane, so our adventures have been long car trips. We have been to forty national parks including Glacier, Yellowstone, and the Grand Tetons. We've traveled with my sister Merdi and her husband, Tom to the western states where the scenery is like another world. I bought hiking sticks and practiced using them in Bryce Canyon National Park, the Grand Tetons, and the Grand Canyon. During these long drives, we never argue or have any disagreements except for one thing. I've told David that anyone who drives the speed limit ought to get off the road. Those times when he is really poking along, his foot barely gracing the gas pedal, I have made him pull over so I can take the wheel and get to our destination more quickly.

Ever since I had graduated from college I had the dream

to drive the Alaskan Highway. But driving round trip to Alaska from Dallas seemed out of the question. After doing some research we figured out a way we could drive an RV from Elkhart, Indiana, to Alaska, then fly home. In Elkhart, David and I picked up a brand-new RV. Looking at that great, big, shiny beast I wondered if we were crazy. How could we possibly think we were capable of maneuvering this ten-ton vehicle hundreds of miles into the wilderness? Taking risks was not one of my strong suits. As I inspected the interior of our new home on wheels, I tried to give myself courage by reminding myself of a great regret in life.

After I graduated from college, I imagined myself signing up with Volunteers in Service to America (VISTA), a government organization that places qualified teachers into low-income neighborhoods around the country including Alaska. It would have been a two-year commitment in a school district where poverty was plentiful and opportunity scarce. But I could not find the courage to take such a risk, and to this day, it is one of my greatest regrets. Since then, I have owned my lack of risk-taking with the promise that I would try to do better. This trip to Alaska, something that David encouraged me to do, sent a thrill through me even though we were venturing into the great unknown.

David and I have been together for over 12 years and married for almost 9 years. Dave and I were married 33 years. Many people do not have one happy marriage and I feel fortunate that I have enjoyed the love of two men.

13

TRAILBLAZER

Over 40 years have passed since I began my career teaching children and adults with special needs. With each step, mistake, and small victory, I have seen how education and communication have changed lives. People who were once considered throwaways are now productive, responsible, and happy members of our communities. But this is a critical moment for these young adults who stand at the precipice of life. Every day I am compelled to make certain that in the coming years, young people have resources such as person-centered planning to launch them into their futures.

So much of what I have witnessed since the start of my career in special education has been revolutionary. It feels similar to the experience of watching the world progress from candlelight to electricity, from horse carriages to rocket ships, from snail mail to email. I have worked in special education before there were laws that mandated its existence. I have seen the ugliness of prejudice against people and children with disabilities. But I focus on the progress that has been made in this country, where today things like wheelchair access are normalized.

From 2008 to 2010, I was saddled with the worst boss I had ever worked with. She made my life miserable. There were no hopeful signs that her days on the job were numbered. But I knew that with her above me, I would not last until my projected retirement date.

All the while, in the back of my mind, I harbored an idea. But it felt disjointed like it was more of a pipe dream than something that could become a reality. The idea was still sitting on that proverbial shelf where I had laid it for safekeeping when my dear friend Vicki had gotten sick. What if I took it from the shelf, dusted it off, and revived the idea of opening my own business? A business where I consulted with families who needed guidance for their children with disabilities. Where I could put together person-centered plans for individuals who were no longer in the education system but needed direction? I wanted to work with school districts to help other educators learn innovative ways to provide quality instruction so that they could discover the giftedness of their students leading to an inclusive life in their communities. I had no idea how to go about starting a business, and I was not completely confident that my idea had merit. Then it hit me. I needed to put together a person-centered plan for myself!

I gathered my troops—my friend Terri and other friends

who were lawyers and educators, and my family members. I reached out to people who knew my financial situation. I even invited my contacts at the University of Texas, the Arc of Dallas, and the University of Kansas. My friend Ann O'Brian, Luke's mom, said to me, "Debbie your plan is missing something – your spirituality." I was touched and honored to have Ann take on that role.

We came together at my home. I had whiteboards scattered about the room. Not only did the group get down to the nitty-gritty of my personality and my capabilities, but we also delved into creating a business plan for my new venture. My friend Noreen Gill facilitated the meeting. Later Terri said that the meeting felt like a retreat where my life was under a loving and supportive microscope.

Before launching any sort of business, I had to look at my finances. Somehow everything was falling into place. I was close to fulfilling my 30 years of service, so my retirement was assured. I determined what I would receive in retirement. If I lived off the lesser amount for a year I would be able to save the difference to back my future venture.

Back at my school, my boss was really showing her ugly colors and it seemed like her mission was to get rid of me. Because I wanted to care for Dave during his final days, I had accumulated and set aside all my sick days planning for that time. But Dave had died before I could even take that time off. I was able to step away from school and use those days designing the materials that would later become the center of my new business. Then I got an offer that made my head spin.

Judith was a friend of mine who worked for Northeast ISD. She had hired me to do a few person-centered trainings for their staff. She knew how unhappy I was at my job in the Richardson ISD. One day Judith called and offered me a job in her school district! The job offer was a huge step with a much higher salary than I was making. I thought long and hard about it. Then I called Judith with my decision. I could not take the job. I knew if I committed to a new employer, I would want to stay for a minimum of five years. But the desire to launch my own business had been ignited in my brain and there was no way I was going to place it on that dusty shelf again.

Instead of my becoming a paid staff person at her school district, Judith contracted me to train her staff to provide person-centered planning and evaluate the vocational and transition program in the district. This led to me facilitating a system's change with secondary programming in the district. Along with Judith, I made a presentation at a statewide conference for special education directors. That led to me giving talks at other conferences. I soon was recognized as a leader in the area of transition, vocational training, and self-determination and presented at over 20 state-wide and regional conferences a year.

My life became a whirlwind. I was traveling across the state, doing trainings, and presenting at conferences. I was dating David, learning about this new man and how serious our intentions might become with each other. My mother, looking at my life, said that she had never seen me so fulfilled but warned me to take time off so that I could nurture the relationship with David.

In 2010 I established DR Wilkes Consulting with the tagline "Building a Promising Future." My philosophy was that everyone is born with gifts and talents that should be nurtured and appreciated by the world at large. I believe in a supreme being, and I know that my God does not make mistakes. We are all made in his/her likeness. What better way to understand God's gifts than to find and appreciate the giftedness in all people? I do not understand the emphasis on the first three letters in the word "disability." We need to take time to see the "ABILITIES" in all of us.

To do this, I offered my clientele a menu of services ranging from person-centered planning and the LifeCourse Trajectory to workshops covering self-determination, vocational training, interdependence, alternatives to guardianship, and inclusion. I also consulted to review existing programs helping administrators evaluate and improve, the services that they offer to students with disabilities. Along with an attorney I created a tool to help parents and teachers prepare students to become more independent and have less need for guardianship.

My business fulfilled my central passion—helping young people transition from their school years into their adult years. The plans we created for them followed the idea that they can have a "Good Life" and avoid their worst nightmares. Parents were an integral part of my coaching— their efforts and expectations were incorporated as we planned their children's futures.

Some of the ideas included in my presentations felt like plain old common sense. The question arose wondering how a classroom with one teacher and a paraprofessional with seven students, each with different skill sets, could possibly foster the abilities of seven different people inside a single working environment? The answer seemed simple. For example, if a funeral home agreed to train students, did this mean that only the single student who desired to work in a funeral home should take advantage of this job site? Not a chance, I said. Within that funeral home, one student could learn about clerical work. Another student could practice cleaning and straightening public spaces. A third student could handle flower arrangements and a fourth could be trained to do landscaping and horticulture. This one job site that seems to be a small niche, could be used to train a wide variety of skills.

This technique can be misunderstood. The students being placed together at a job site deserve a sense of dignity. One time while I was working at a school in Cedar Hill, Texas, I went to observe a pizza parlor job site in their program. What I saw broke my heart. Sitting around a table were four students putting together pizza boxes. The worst thing for these students and customers is for them to believe that it requires several of them to accomplish one task – a task that likely three out of the four were uninterested in.

The students should have a clear understanding of the skills that they are learning and how that will translate into their "dream job". Another day while at an Office Depot job site run by the Northeast ISD I encountered a student who was very belligerent. I approached him and said, "You seem so unhappy. What is it about this place?" Scornfully he said, "I want to work in a movie theater! I don't know why they have me here!" I said, "Okay, but look at the job skills you are learning here that you can take with you when you work at a movie theater. At the theater, you might be behind the concessions counter. You will need to know how to re-stock all those candies and drinks. You will need to know how to direct people to the correct movie. Can you tell me where to find the printing cartridges?"

Proudly the young man led me to the cartridges and asked me how many I needed. Then he seemed to calm down. Just explaining to him how what he was learning would bring him to his goal helped remotivate and redirect him to the task at hand.

My friend Shelley Dumas, who I had studied with at McGill University, had left teaching to get her doctorate at the University of Texas at Austin. Along with Jeff Garrison-Tate and Laura Bukner they created a learning community for people and agency representatives who were interested in person-centered thinking. When Shelly called asking for my help to expand the interest to teachers and school administrators, I didn't have to think twice. Using skills developed by Michael Smull and the Learning Community it took me over three years to create a process called Person-Centered Transition Assessment. Through the development process, I recorded over 200 hours of facilitating person-centered plans. Using those recordings, I wrote a guidebook that could reach beyond the borders of Texas to educators everywhere.

As I trained more teachers and hosted more workshops, the assessment process was considered best practices and was shared at national conferences.

TOMMY

While scheduling a two-day training at Northeast ISD, I advised the staff to select a student and their family to participate in a person-centered plan that I would facilitate. I strongly suggested they not choose the toughest case, because although I knew I could handle most any student, the aftereffects might have the staff quaking in their boots, unsure of their own capabilities. Well of course they wanted me to work with the student who had the most significant needs, so my advice went out the window.

When I arrived, the selected student's parents were in the room. But Tommy, their 20-year-old son, was nowhere in sight. I said, "I'm sorry but I cannot do the plan if Tommy is not here." The mother said, "Tommy is napping right now." With a shake of my head, I again told everyone present that the plan can't move forward without Tommy's participation. I said that I was contracted to return in about three months and we could meet then. The mother wanted the assessment and realized that she would have to give in. She agreed to let the school staff leave to get her son. Before receiving too much information about a person, I always want to meet them first, so I was not aware of what Tommy's disability was. When Tommy arrived, I could see that he had a profound intellectual developmental disability and some type of medical condition where he needed round-the-clock nursing.

Tommy was reclined in his wheelchair with his eyes closed. I went over to him then put my face close to his. I said, "Hi Tommy. I'm Debbie and I'm here to talk with you." Tommy's eyes opened and he gave me a big smile. I looked at his parents and said, "So often we make assumptions about what people cannot do. But I am going to do the opposite and assume that Tommy understands that I am here to talk with him."

So, then we got to work. Tommy had earned the academic requirements necessary for graduation. He was receiving services through a Medicaid waiver that provided 24-hour care. I explained to everyone that the school's role is to provide the instruction necessary for him to transition to a good quality of life including employment. Or he can graduate now based on having access to adult services. If he is coming to school to sleep and is not being taught anything, then there is no reason for him to be here. For Tommy to remain in school past the age of 18, the school needed to be teaching him skills for a potential job. If his job prospects are zero, then Tommy's school days would come to an end. What then?

Tommy's mother announced that there was no vision for Tommy to work after he graduated from high school. In their minds Tommy's physical needs would be met through the funding they would receive from the state. They had not given any thought to Tommy's individuality as a productive human being – how he could find a job and have a purpose in life. I said bluntly, "So you're telling me that after he graduates, he is just going to be at home with nursing care?" They nodded their heads.

It was time for me to dive into the family's personal life. Perhaps I could uncover a gap that Tommy could fill. Sure enough I learned that the father sat on a parish board for a Catholic church and Tommy's mother was the director of religious education at their church. As we continued to talk, we looked at Tommy to learn his reaction to our discussion. His mother said, "He seems to really like the music at church. I can see him getting excited while it's playing." This was an 'Ah-ha!' moment. I said, "Great! Because you take him to Mass each Sunday maybe Tommy could become a greeter.

His presence could be seen, and he would have a purpose." Tommy's mother thought about it then said, "That's a good idea."

Now Tommy had a reason to stay in school. His teachers could work with him on the skill sets he would need to become a greeter. His story showcased for the school staff that they needed to revamp their transition program. They had not seriously looked at employment options for students like Tommy. My message seemed to sink in – we needed to think differently. Although Tommy's job as a greeter at church was not a paid position, we had the opportunity to improve his quality of life by giving him a purpose. At the same time, we would be teaching parishioners how to include Tommy at church.

* * *

Traversing the state giving my transition training seminars was fulfilling. My own skill set was being used purposefully and I hoped, to make a difference. Financially I was supporting myself beyond my wildest expectations. But I was in for a big disappointment. Months after conducting a training at a particular school district, I heard that none of my methods and processes were ever put into place. The school district paid my fees, allowed me to take up their staff's time giving them cutting-edge ideas on how to reshape their programs, but once I was out the door, nothing changed. Most importantly I had met with students and parents and raised their hopes but nothing changed!

One day after I led a training for a Service Center in Corpus Christi a woman came up to me and said, "I love your presentations! I've been coming to hear you for over five years. I always come to listen to you." I asked her to tell me how she had been using the practices she learned from my presentations. Without missing a beat, she said, "Oh that works for you, but not us. Not our program."

I knew then that I would need to make some changes. No longer would I only communicate with the special education staff when planning a training for them. From now on, before agreeing to train in a district, I would ask the director to identify all of the stakeholders. To be successful I would expect to train teachers, para-professionals, administrators, and parents. The principals and other school administrators would need to see the value and relevance of what I was bringing to the staff. If the superintendent knew what those precious budget dollars were being spent on, he or she would not let it go to waste. I hoped that this would give my trainings life once I departed.

Due to the pandemic and my experience providing staff developments, and perhaps my age, I changed my business plan. I now no longer give trainings or facilitate system changes, and instead provide individual support to people with disabilities from the age of 6 to 58. I help plan a positive future for the individual and continue to coach them to succeed. People want to label me and call me a counselor, a transition consultant, and a life coach. Just as Karen had said years ago, "We label jars, not people." I am a person who believes that everyone has gifts, talents, and a purpose. I just try to help everyone appreciate these qualities in each other.

14

LIFE AFTER THE CLASSROOM

I n Texas, adults with disabilities can be vulnerable to guardianship laws. Guardianship should be the last resort as a solution to someone's care. Once guardianship is granted, common rights such as voting, driving, marriage, and making healthcare decisions are taken away. The only population that is comparable in having their rights removed are convicted prisoners.

I was quoted on this topic in an article about guardianship on www.SpecialEdConnection.com: "The minute (parents) do guardianship, you are really disaffirming the idea of self-determination. Some teachers don't realize that guardianship totally conflicts with IEP goals that we put in place to promote self-determination and self-advocacy skills." I was further quoted: "I'm not going to say that guardianship should never be done – I think there are times when parents should have guardianship."

For guardianship to be approved, a person must be incapacitated, unable to understand information, or make and communicate decisions. The person is unable to assume their physical care and safety without the aid of another person. I have always stressed that even under guardianship, family members should attempt at every opportunity to allow the person to help make self-determining decisions. Alternatives to guardianship include Power of Attorney, and, in Texas, Supported Decision Making. Once guardianship is awarded it will not be revoked until the ward goes back to court to prove his or her competency.

It is typically family members who apply for guardianship of a person who is disabled. All guardianships are facilitated through the courts. This means attorneys must be hired and a judge has the final say. Should a judge determine that the person is 'incapacitated' or disabled, and guardianship is necessary, the person becomes a ward.

I have always believed in the dignity of risk. Everyone, whether disabled or not, makes choices and decisions all having a degree of risk. Mistakes will be made, and victories will happen. But the outcomes are some of the best life lessons that make us stronger and wiser. Taking away the ability to make decisions removes part of a person's autonomy.

Interdependence, where we lean on the assistance of those we trust in life, or we use services necessary for our well-being without giving up our independence, goes away should one be made a ward and receive guardianship. I worry that too many guardianships are inappropriately approved not for protective purposes but because the person has a disability. Society tends to lean towards believing that persons with disabilities are incapable of living a regular life, making their own decisions, and managing life. There is an amount of prejudice in these perceptions. The more people with disabilities are out in society, the more people will come to realize how capable they are. This is how acceptance can take place.

A prominent attorney named Rick found out about the life planning and person-centered plans I did for my clients. A primary area of his business was guardianships. One time he asked me about my thoughts on guardianships. I said, "Guardianship is the most intrusive thing you can do to anyone. You are taking all their rights away." There was no ambiguity in my answer. Rick knew where I stood.

Still, he referred many families to me including the young woman who became a dog groomer – Logan. Throughout the process of developing Logan's person-centered plan, I was in total disagreement that she be put under guardianship. But it wasn't my call. Logan requested and the court ruled in Logan and her family's favor, making Logan a ward and giving her family the power to make all the decisions affecting her life.

Logan's family referred me to friends of theirs who had a son named Ben with disabilities caused by a closed head injury. At one time, Ben had tried to take his own life. When the time came for Ben to leave the rehabilitation center, the family sought legal guardianship. Rick was the attorney drawing up and filing the papers on behalf of the parents. In Dallas county, a person from the courts visits with the potential ward and evaluates the individual to determine if guardianship is appropriate. After the visit, it was decided that Ben should be his own guardian. Rick called me to ask my opinion.

My response surprised him. I said, "This is a slam dunk." In my mind, this was a rare case where guardianship was necessary, and having it could save Ben's life. I added, "Absolutely the family should have guardianship." According to Rick, having this opinion made me a powerful witness. He asked if I would testify in court on behalf of his clients.

In the courtroom, while I sat in the witness chair, Rick asked me several questions all to show the judge that I was against guardianship in general. I told the judge that I am on the board of directors of the Arc of Texas; that I support self-advocacy for people with disabilities. Then Rick asked, "How do you feel about guardianships?" I said, "I don't think people should have guardianship unless it is totally necessary." Then the judge looked down at me and said, "What do you think about Ben's family having guardianship?" My answer was that yes, they should receive guardianship.

I've never believed in pigeonholing a population of people. We can't create policies that have no fluidity. In my profession, the personalities, talents, and characteristics of my students and clients are a kaleidoscope of color. Person-centered planning digs deep into the features of a person. And when it comes to guardianships as much as I don't like the way the law is written, there are times when it is necessary.

* * *

Over 40 years ago I had stepped into my first classroom and in one day, flew through my entire month of lesson plans. How could I have ever thought that a newly graduated teacher knew enough to be so confident? On that morning, my first day of teaching, when the ringing of the starting bell echoed across the school grounds, my own education was just beginning. I've learned more inside the classroom than I could have if 15 college degrees were hanging on my wall. My students were my professors, and my co-workers were my advisors. Helping to find answers to the dilemmas of my students was like an incubator of learning.

I also credit the cutting-edge information I learned at McGill University. Many of the concepts such as inclusion are now ingrained in my philosophy. I've attended dozens of workshops from where I gleaned forward-thinking methods that I put into practice with my students. The Institute for Person-Centered Practices taught me how to synthesize a person's needs to give them a quality of life using 'important to' and 'important for.' In so many cases, compassionate people wanting to help another person will fall all over themselves advising what is important *for* that person completely forgetting to ask what is important *to* that person.

The Institute for Person-Centered Practices taught me a core concept of person-centered thinking: Balancing "Important TO" and "Important FOR." Important To includes the things that make a person happy including places, people, routines, material things. Important FOR are the people, routines, things, medications that help a person with wellness, have a sense of dignity, and freedom of fear. When explaining this concept I relate it to weight loss. Many people are overweight because food is Important TO them. Losing weight is Important FOR them and they don't lose weight. No one will do something that is important for them unless it is important to them. Through soulful listening and creative thinking, we can help people get a balance. David and I had been dating for 2 years and he went to a session that I was presenting to parents. Later that evening he told me that he understood that I have been using that concept as we were dating. I think if everyone would consider this concept, all our relationships would improve.

People talking to each other to express opinions and ideas is stimulating and moves us forward. But what if a person does not have language? The Institute for Person-Centered Practices has developed a Communication Chart that can be used to support someone who doesn't use words. There are four components:

What is happening

When this happens I do this

What I think it means

I want you to support me by

There was a time I was working with a young man in San Antonio. Occasionally he would use his right hand to do a chopping motion against his neck. Then, when ignored, he would hit the desk or any person who came near him. The meaning behind this behavior was hard to understand because he would only do it periodically. While facilitating a person-centered plan with him and his family we learned that what he was trying to communicate was that he had a sore throat. Just imagine how difficult it must have been for him when he was trying to tell his teachers that he was hurting and was being ignored? No wonder he became more upset lashing out at people and things.

* * *

After having spent decades in the classroom, working with hundreds of students, I may have left part of my heart in those unforgettable years. But the work I have done since then has sustained me. I have consulted all over the state of Texas helping with special education programs. I continue to coach inclusion, self-advocacy, and transitioning of young adults into their "adulting" years. I fully believe in the vast potential of the people I have counseled. By nurturing their talents and skills to life, more and more people in the general population will come to discover and appreciate the many abilities that my clients have.

Thankfully, today I am seeing new approaches to fostering independence while work opportunities for people with disabilities are expanding. But there is still so much work that needs to be done. Most of the person-centered planning done today are within agencies that are uncreative in their approach and do not really listen to the person. They work to fit the person into the system rather than figuring out how to make the system work to help the person realize their dreams.

Private consultants like myself are few and far between. It is imperative that others in my field pick up the reins and provide these services to people far beyond Texas. Although systems keep changing I am not sure if they are improving. School systems are expected to prepare all students for the adult world. There are honors and advanced placement classes for a small group of students to be prepared for high-rated universities. What if the same effort was put into helping students with disabilities to be better prepared for their adult world? What if we all worked together to create a community where all people were welcomed and included.

Parents too should reach for the stars for their kids who have a disability. So often I've seen parents who are scared to have imagination when it comes to the life their child can have beyond school. Everyone deserves to have a purposeful life, and if parents and educators get behind the effort to provide a quality curriculum and job training through special education programs, both the students and their parents will have a higher quality of life after graduation.

At age 18, a student of mine named student Charles had moved from Wisconsin with his family to the Richardson ISD in Texas. Wisconsin law provides special education services through age 25 and Charles' parents expected the same for him in Texas. In Richardson, after a student meets their academic requirements for graduation, the instructional programming changes to focus on skills for employment. School services for the student end after the student's 21st year.

Charles had arrived with enough academic credits that I thought we could place him right into our transition program. But his parents disagreed. They pointed out that Charles was in the band and that they wanted him to make new friends. Their wish was for him to remain in school as long as possible, just as he would have if they were in Wisconsin.

Bobbie was my boss at the time. She worried that since our program was so new and innovative, and even though we had proposed a solid Individual Education plan for Charles if the parents submitted a grievance against the district, the Texas Education Agency might side with the family which could hurt our program.

We allowed Charles to remain at the high school for an extra year and shortened his time in the Transition Program. As a result, he lacked some of the opportunities to prepare him for the adult world. Years after he graduated, I spoke with his mother who said to me, "It was such a mistake on our part to not allow enough time to prepare Charles." I commiserated with her that the lack of time really stunted our efforts on Charles's behalf.

NICK

Nick, born with Down Syndrome, had a lot of ideas about his future. He and his parents Katie and Paul came to me in January of 2012 for a person-centered plan where we could flesh out a place for him in the world. Although Nick loved the idea of being a radio disc jockey, later he decided that was just a hobby. Over the next few years, Nick worked at a restaurant and a retail store. The experiences were valuable in giving him a clear picture of what he wanted his career to look like.

Nick loved Ford Mustangs. He learned about a local Ford dealership that partnered with several high schools' "Life Skills" programs that offer students with special needs ways to learn independence. Nick interviewed with the dealership and was hired. His shift was in the afternoons, Monday through Friday. He worked cleaning cars and making sure the customer lounge was properly stocked and tidy.

Nick became an essential employee at the dealership. The work he did was not something the company offered him for charitable reasons. He was an important part of the staff doing a job that was vital to the quality of service the dealership takes pride in. Because Nick is a visual learner, Nick's boss provided him with a workbook of instructions, an illustration of the dealership's floorplan, and photos of the staff to help him remember names. Sometimes Nick feels frustrated with himself when he has trouble forming his words, but that has not stopped him from making friends with the other employees. For his birthday, the staff threw Nick a birthday party with cake and a game of football.

Nick's parents are so proud of their son. They saw how his choices were making a difference for himself, learning how to be independent, interacting with new people, being responsible for a job well done. And he was making a good salary too! His parents also knew first-hand that the vibe at the dealership was very positive. In the past they had purchased a car there for their other son, so they knew the workplace would be safe and supportive to Nick.

One employee in a Ford community service video said of Nick, "He's my brother. I told him to make sure to come to tell me if he has any trouble. He is part of our family." Another employee said, "When I'm down and out and I see Nick, he puts a smile on my face. He's a loving guy."

15

MY GRANDCHILDREN

"The secret of happiness is to live moment by moment and to thank God for all that He, in His goodness, sends to us day after day."

-St Gianna Molla

In August 2015 came the birth of my granddaughter, Caroline. She was born with a rare genetic condition with various implications including nonverbal autism, low muscle tone, and cognitive impairment. My entire career has been focused on making the world more accepting and usable for those with disabilities. I imagined that I knew almost everything in my field. But this little girl has taught me so much more. Now I know first-hand what it is like to walk in the shoes of family members advocating for their loved ones. She has validated my belief that God does not make mistakes.

I have four grandchildren. Harper and Caroline are Beth's girls, and Jamille has David and Mary. These four little people are my everything. My husband David says he's never seen or experienced anyone making as big an effort to be a part of their grandchildren's lives as I have. During the time of Covid with in-person visits risky and rare, I want my grandchildren to know who I am in the most significant way possible. David chuckles knowing that my grandson David is going to outgrow me soon. But at this point, he genuinely seems to like hanging out with me.

My grandchildren are still so young, but when they were babies, I wondered if as they grew up, would they be kind? Would they figure out ways to help others before thinking of themselves? In the years ahead when I am long out of the workforce, would my grandchildren take over, making discoveries that could further the understanding of overlooked populations?

But already I am seeing selflessness in them – so much so that two of them are lessening the worrier in me. Caroline's older sister Harper feels so responsible for her little sister. She has told me that when she grows up, she will take care of Caroline. I am overwhelmed seeing her compassion for her sister, but I want Harper to live her own life too. To that end, when Caroline was born, I set up a special needs trust for her to ensure that she receives care so that both she and Harper can achieve their potential.

Mary is six years old and already has revealed her heart of gold. Recently she was being bullied by a boy in her class. She described her feelings to her mother: "It's so hard because my heart hurts for him because he's going through something to be so mean to everybody so I'm trying to be nice but then he called me stupid and I got mad." How does a six-year-old have such a keen sense about the troubles of another? Especially someone who is treating her so badly. This empathy is evident in all my grandchildren.

Jamille's family describes these gifts as superpowers. She says our superpowers are God's power in us. She also says that even I have superpowers! The ability I have to harness my gifts and put them to work and to know I don't have all the answers. But as Jamille remembers, those early days at CTC when she watched me pushing boulders up mountains, trying to convince the higher-ups that inclusion was not a scary word, I was God's instrument.

David, now 10 years old, is a kind, old soul. He loves to play sports and have fun, but he is sensitive to the thoughts and feelings of others. With a family filled with girls, I have made an extra effort to connect with my only grandson. He asks questions that show the depth of his concern about others. He seeks understanding about his cousin Caroline. I've watched him bend his head close to hers, their eyes locking, sharing smiles. Their connection is genuine. He has no fear of Caroline because he gets her. And Caroline adores David.

When my four grandchildren are together, they dream up the most imaginative games. Whether they pretend to be operating a restaurant or are in a spy movie trying to save the world, there is always a role for Caroline. On a recent visit to my house, they created an entire restaurant in our playroom. Harper, the maître d' greeted her first customer, David. She seated him at his table then rattled off the menu items – Macaroni & Cheese, salmon, and pizza. David selected the salmon. Meanwhile, the two chef's Caroline and Mary were in the kitchen where playdough was their main ingredient. With plastic knives, the two girls cut and fashioned the playdough into what they imagine looked like salmon steaks. Harper served David with a flourish, and he dug into his dish. Later, he signed his name on a piece of paper, included a tip, and left the restaurant a satisfied customer.

When they play the spy game, Caroline is the super-secret agent. Her mission is to find the high-tech gadget that will save the world from destruction. One time, Caroline figured that the gadget was in the laundry room. After searching there for a bit, she returned to her cohorts with a cloth that she found. They congratulated her on completing her mission! Only a super-secret agent could have figured out that something as low-tech as a piece of material could have led to a world disaster.

Harper at 10 years old, was my second grandchild. She's filled with creativity and hopes to be an actress or fashion designer when she grows up. To prepare herself for these ventures, she and her little sister Caroline often play dress-up. Caroline has a Barbie Doll Make-up table where they spend hours applying makeup, dressing each other in costumes, and imagining themselves as other people in made-up worlds.

These two girls have a sisterhood that is special yet ordinary. They might have a squabble here or there, but Caroline is very in tune with Harper's feelings. When Harper is upset or angry, Caroline wants to comfort her. Because of Covid, their parents have relied on Harper to help more around the house. She will make breakfast for Caroline and is the one who figures out activities the two girls can do together. They both equally enjoy taking their dogs to the dog park or swimming in their pool, so arguing is rare between them. The girls love flowers. A visit to a Dallas Arboretum where they can see varieties of exotic flowers, filling up their lungs with the aroma of a million scents, and taking off their shoes to wade in the brook, is a magical, shared experience. They also enjoy cooking together. Harper's specialties are making muffins and cakes while Caroline is the salad chef.

I try to spend one-on-one time with each of my four grandchildren. Harper and I enjoy riding our bikes together. Sometimes we will map our ride to a fun destination to motivate us to get a good workout. A nearby ice-cream parlor usually does the trick.

One night when David was eight years old, he and I were lying on his bed with a book propped up between us. It was a young reader's book titled Out of My Mind by Sharon

Draper. We were taking turns reading each page out loud. The story was about a 12-year-old girl named Melody who was born with cerebral palsy. Because she cannot talk or take care of herself most everyone believes she is stupid. But tucked inside her body lives a girl with amazing abilities. She has a brilliant mind with a photographic memory. David was enthralled with the story because it reminded him of his cousin Caroline.

When he was asked what he thought about the book, David said, "I kind of felt sorry for Melody. She reminded me of Caroline because she is so intelligent, but she just can't really show it. I think Caroline is smart, but she can't really express it." Caroline hugs David or uses sign language to tell him things. He talks to her in normal tones, never using 'baby talk' because as he puts it, "Every time someone did a baby voice to her (Caroline) it would just be a reminder that I'm different. So, I include her as normally as possible." Someone once asked David if he could tell the whole world how to treat people with disabilities what he would say: "Try to treat them as normally as possible and to include them too."

Just after Caroline was born, I visited her in the NICU. We would have to touch her to wake her up for her feedings. She was so tiny, and I worried that my cold hands would startle her. But as my eyes swept across her precious body, I could feel my love for her filling me up inside. I prayed to God that she was not suffering and that she would thrive.

After all these years devoted to educating, advising, and advocating for people with disabilities I now felt as if I was sharing in their experience. We were in for a rocky but not impassable road ahead. God had given us this little girl for a reason.

It was my turn to read a page from our book, but before I had finished, David stopped me. He said, "Melody and Caroline are a lot alike." Then with a worried look on his face, he said, "Will she get treated the way Melody was?" So, I began to tell him stories about my students and about Mia who had cerebral palsy but who was now an accomplished young woman. With excitement, David sat up. He said, "G! (He calls me G instead of Grandma), you need to write this story down! People need to know this!" He was right. The character of Melody was dismissed as a person of any worth by so many people around her. Once they saw first-hand her many capabilities, their attitudes changed.

My students had to overcome the same misconceptions by working even harder than everyone else. It would be so helpful to them if their lives and experiences were given to the world. If people could gain an understanding and find compassion for those who are different from them, the Melody's of the world could find unlimited opportunities. I don't have all the answers that could sweep away the rocks and boulders from the road Caroline will travel on. But we must keep our minds and hearts open and be receptive to ideas that come our way. We must take the time to listen to what a child is telling us. As hard as I've championed my students as they've leaped over life's hurdles, my granddaughter Caroline has pushed my faith even further.

I remember going to Kansas City where my daughter Beth and her husband had settled. In their living room, I watched baby Caroline laying on the floor with her occupational therapist nearby. The therapist exclaimed at her progress. Yet I thought to myself, "God help me see it because right now I don't." I sat there sending up silent prayers asking God to let her walk. Please let her walk.

As she grew, Caroline began to use a small walker. That child had so much determination! Once she no longer needed the walker, she figured out how to go up and down stairs. Then one day I watched as she moved across the yard towards the swing set. When she got to a dangling swing, she grasped onto the ropes on either side of the seat and pulled herself up. All by herself, she was able to get herself onto that seat. She knew exactly what she wanted, and through her own efforts, she achieved it. The swing began to move slowly back and forth and the joy that lit up her face reminded me of that day when she was a baby. My prayers had been answered.

When Caroline started school, she had her first IEP. She was unable to use words to communicate so I knew it was important that we teach her the first step towards self-advocacy, the power to say "no." Looking at her behavior, we noticed that she would put both of her hands to her ears. We thought she could be telling us "No" but we believed it also meant other things. We had to look at the behavior along with what was happening in that exact moment. Each time an airplane passed overhead she would do this behavior. So, we thought she must be telling us that she liked airplanes. To further her love for airplanes my husband, my son-in-law and I took Caroline and Harper to an air show. What a disaster! She sat in her stroller screaming the whole time! This was one of those moments of self-reflection when I confirmed that no, I do not have all the answers. I could feel my heart clench with fear and worry.

Years earlier one Sunday at church I noticed a little boy sitting nearby. I knew he had a disability and the smile that lit up his face glowed with happiness. When mass was over, I approached the mother of the boy and said to her, "Your child is an ambassador of friendship. His smile just radiates." After that, my girls teased me constantly, no matter if I was grumpy or in a lighter mood they would say, "Mom you are just an Ambassador of Friendship."

When Beth had trouble finding Caroline a daycare that would accept her, I stepped in to help. Trying to remain optimistic I put on my proverbial Ambassador of Friendship hat while contacting daycares. Then one day while I was taking care of Caroline and she was using her walker as we toured a local mall, I noticed a woman staring at her. This was the last straw, I thought. I had become so sick and tired of people looking at Caroline and wondering what is "wrong" with her. The Ambassador of Friendship hat had flown off my head.

I stared back at the woman and said to her as if in explanation, "She has autism."

The woman said, "I can see that she is doing the best she can."

"I wish other people would see that because her mother can't seem to find a daycare program that will take her," I said.

"Oh really?" the woman responded, "I work for a daycare, and I've worked with children with autism for years. I bet my daycare will accept her."

he was right. The daycare program accepted Caroline. My fear and worry for Caroline's future did not stop me from speaking about her with perfect strangers. Maybe a little bit of the Ambassador of Friendship helped to calm me down enough to be civilized which led to such a wonderful outcome. Because while Caroline was in the daycare program, she was invited to birthday parties and made friends.

One day I went with Caroline and her school to an All-Ability Park where the activities are tailor-made for kids with special needs. The playgrounds have synthetic turf that makes it easy for wheelchairs and walkers; easy to access merry-go-rounds and climbing structures, all with color-coded difficulty level signage. Caroline was using her walker when a little boy came up to us and started talking to her. Then he turned to me and said, "Caroline is in my kindergarten class, but she can't talk."

I could feel myself getting emotional. "Yes, right," I said to him.

"But I understand her," he said.

Later I approached a woman who I believed was his mother. I said, "Is that your son over there?" She got a worried expression on her face, so I continued, "I just want to tell you how wonderful he is." Then I described to her how kind he was to my granddaughter who has autism.

"Oh, he has an older brother with autism," she said.

We then started talking about her older son and the support services she had for him. Before we parted, she asked for my phone number. In the coming weeks, she and I spoke a few times and I was able to give her some leads that could help her older son. Then recently she sent me a text that said: "My younger son is having a birthday party and he told me he would not have the party without Caroline there. Can you please give me Caroline's mother's phone number so I can send her an invitation?" The weekend of that party Caroline was very busy because she had not one, but two birthday parties to attend with classmates in her general education kindergarten class.

There was a time when I would not talk about Caroline's disability out of respect for her parents. It was not my story to tell. But together we discussed this until Beth and Ryan gave me permission to talk to others about Caroline and her diagnosis. I wonder though if there will ever come a day when people spot Caroline in a store, a restaurant, at the library, and they don't bat an eye, not staring, not questioning. Because I think that is what acceptance will look like. Caroline will just be noticed for just being a human being.

I constantly think about the future – what does it hold for my grandchildren? What about the people who I have served these many years? Whenever I begin working with a new client, what answers will come to me that will help them to have a fulfilling life? Observation has always served me well. Keeping my mind and heart open, asking the Holy Spirit to lead me, and receiving my faith in God pulls me in the direction I must go. As much as I've tried to make a difference for my students and young clients, I know that I am just one woman working within a system that can move like a glacier. But whether I experience a setback or a victory I think of the starfish story:

One day a man was walking along the beach when he noticed a boy hurriedly picking up and gently throwing things into the ocean. Approaching the boy, he asked, "Young man, what are you doing?" The boy replied, "Throwing starfish back into the ocean. The surf is up and the tide is going out. If I don't throw them back, they'll die." The man laughed to himself and said, "Don't you realize there are miles and miles of beach and hundreds of starfish? You can't make any difference!"

After listening politely, the boy bent down, picked up another starfish, and threw it into the surf. Then, smiling at the man, he said, **"I made a difference to that one."**
adapted from *The Star Thrower* by Loren Eiseley

I will never claim to be an expert or to have all the answers. But never wavering from the belief that everyone is a gift from God empowers me to underscore how we are all equals. My sister Janet says that I am the most non-judgmental person she knows. Because I don't overlay my perceptions onto people, maybe that is why I know in my heart that no matter who you are, the sky is the limit.

THE END

"You are the everlasting light.

Help me bring Your love everywhere I go.

Penetrate and possess my whole being so that all my life will be a radiance of You.

Shine through me and be so in me that everyone I come in contact with today may feel Your presence in my spirit.

Let them look and see, not just me, but YOU. Light of lights shining through me."

-Adapted from John Cardinal Newman's prayer

Harper and Caroline

David and Mary

Story Terrace

Made in the USA
Columbia, SC
17 May 2022

60550997R00114